James Croil, John Jenkins, Alexander Mathieson

The Life of the Rev. Alexander Mathieson

James Croil, John Jenkins, Alexander Mathieson

The Life of the Rev. Alexander Mathieson

ISBN/EAN: 9783337375034

Printed in Europe, USA, Canada, Australia, Japan

Cover: Foto ©Lupo / pixelio.de

More available books at **www.hansebooks.com**

LIFE

OF THE

Rev. Alex. Mathieson, D.D.

MINISTER OF ST. ANDREW'S CHURCH, MONTREAL;

WITH A

Funeral Sermon,

BY THE REV JOHN JENKINS, D.D.,

MINISTER OF ST. PAUL'S CHURCH, MONTREAL;

AND

Three Discourses,

PREACHED BY DR. MATHIESON, AT DIFFERENT PERIODS OF HIS MINISTRY.

Quod potui perfeci.

MONTREAL:
DAWSON BROTHERS, ST. JAMES STREET.
1870.

This Work,

UNDERTAKEN AT THE INSTANCE OF

ALEXANDER BUNTIN, ESQ.,

OF MONTREAL,

IS RESPECTFULLY

Dedicated

TO

THE MEMBERS OF

ST. ANDREW'S CHURCH AND CONGREGATION,

BY

James Croil,

INTRODUCTION.

These Memoirs of the late Minister of St. Andrew's Church, Montreal, are almost entirely composed of domestic annals, intended rather for the perusal of his numerous personal friends than for general circulation. Had Dr. Mathieson thought it necessary to leave any instructions to his biographer, these would, in all probability, have been, substantially, in terms of the stern command of Oliver Cromwell to an artist when taking his likeness.—"*Paint me, scars, warts, wrinkles and all!*" In our own opinion, the weaker points in the character of our deceased Friend and Father but served to bring out in bolder relief the many noble qualities of the man: therefore, we have not endeavoured to conceal them. If we have failed to produce that which—on the whole—will be recognized as a faithful portraiture, we can only take shelter under the motto that is placed on the title page. In addition to the materials supplied by Dr. Mathieson himself, the author has received much valuable assistance from friends who neither wish nor expect a more particular acknowledgment.

CONTENTS.

Part I.

CHAPTER I.
Parentage and early Education.. 9

CHAPTER II.
College Career and Tutorship.. 22

CHAPTER III.
Recollections of Dr. Chalmers and Edward Irving............................. 32

CHAPTER IV.
Appointment to St. Andrew's Church. His ordination and departure for Canada. 47

CHAPTER V.
Visit to Scotland and the Continent. Disappointment and visionary plans. His marriage. Death of his child 64

CHAPTER VI.
Parish work. Revisits Scotland. Death of Mrs. Mathieson. Life at Beechridge. Death of Janet Ewing Mathieson................................ 80

CHAPTER VII.
Reminiscences. Mr. Bethune. Bishop Strachan. Messrs. Spark, Harkness, Connell. History of St. Andrew's Church.......................... 100

CONTENTS.

CHAPTER VIII.
PAGE

Dr. Mathieson as a Member of Synod... 119

CHAPTER IX.

Last illness and death. Funeral services. Extracts from Dr. Barclay's sermon and other sources.. 155

FUNERAL SERMON. 185

Part II.

SERMONS
By Rev. Alexander Mathieson, D.D.

SERMON I.
" Brethren, pray for us, that the word of the Lord may have *free* course, and be glorified."—II Thessalonians, iii, 1... 207

SERMON II.
" God created man in his own image, in the image of God created he him; male and female created he them. And God blessed them, and God said unto them, Be fruitful and multiply, and replenish the earth, and subdue it: and have dominion over the fish of the sea, and over the fowl of the air, and over every living thing that moveth upon the earth."—Genesis i. 27, 28..... 225

SERMON III.
" And it was winter."—John x, 22.. 245

Friend after friend departs ;
    Who hath not lost a friend ?
There is no union here of hearts
    That finds not here an end !
Were this frail world our final rest,
Living or dying, none were bless'd.

Beyond the flight of time,—
    Beyond the reign of death,—
There surely is some blessed clime,
    Where life is not a breath ;
Nor life's affections transient fire,
Whose sparks fly upward and expire.

There *is* a world above,
    Where parting is unknown ;
A long eternity of love,
    Formed for the good alone ;
And Faith beholds the dying here
Translated to that glorious sphere !

MONTGOMERY.

CHAPTER FIRST.

PARENTAGE AND EARLY EDUCATION.

SOME years ago it occurred to the writer to suggest to Dr. Mathieson that a leisure hour, now and again, might be spent, pleasantly to himself, and usefully to the future historian, in committing to paper some of those early reminiscences of men and things which had often served to beguile hours of social pastime. It seemed right that whatever was in them of historic interest should be rescued from oblivion, and desirable that even trivial occurrences bearing on the history of the Church should be preserved, not necessarily for publication, but as *memorabilia* which might hereafter be used or set aside as should be judged expedient. It was even hinted to him that, without exposing himself to the charge of egotism, he might write an autobiography; for, it was very certain that the time would come when the members of the Church of which he had so long been a minister would naturally seek for all the information that could be had concerning one who, during his later years, was familiarly known to them as the father of the Church of Scotland in Canada. The first part of the proposal was not foreign to the Doctor's habit and bent of mind. He was fond of writing and literally revelled amid the recollections of early days. Indeed, for some years previous to his death he may be said to have been living in the past. Not only had he no sympathy with those changes in ecclesiastic thought which characterize the present time, he could not away with them; he denounced them as " vagaries and innovations " that should not be tolerated, presaging the decay of morals, the downfall of true and undefiled religion, and the utter ruin of—what he maintained to be the only scriptural form of Christianity—Presbyterianism. With regard to his personal history, the idea suggested was one from which his mind intuitively recoiled. He was one of the most modest and unassuming of men, who never in his lifetime coveted the applause of his fellows, nor wished for posthumous praise. Moreover, he was a man of strong mind and yet stronger will, and it can be supposed that in a matter of this kind especially he was not easily influenced; but, as the sequel will show, he yielded to entreaty, rather, doubtless, because of our importunity than from the conviction that compliance were either a virtue or a duty. And though the information eventually arrived at regarding himself is perhaps less full and explicit than we could have wished, it will be seen from the tenor of his own remarks that in this matter, at all events, he was the reverse of " textual." The slightest pretext seemed to him to be sufficient excuse for quite losing sight of himself, and diverging into a lengthened disquisition upon the Paraphrases, the Psalms of David, Dr. Chalmers, Edward Irving, " Harkness," the Union question, or the Organ question: anything, in short, except the particular subject which he had been requested to " stick to." The following extracts from a letter written in 1864, besides corroborating what has been said, are interesting as afford-

PARENTAGE AND EARLY EDUCATION.

ing an insight into the musings of a mind that, to use his own expression, was at times affected with " the doldrums :"

" MY DEAR FRIEND,—

" My last letter was written in such haste and in such an elliptical style that I fear you will require the help of Œdipus to get at its meaning. Mark its deficiencies and send enquiries for the information I have failed to give you. An early friend when he wanted a letter from me—for it would then seem I was sometimes as remiss as I am now—would send me a long string of questions, and tell me to answer them all. You must do the same thing. My memory of by-gone events is not so quick as it once was, and, perhaps, with the dreamings of age I think that every body should be as familiar with the subjects on which I write as I am myself, and I may fail to give that sequence to the narrative that will make it intelligible. Though I delight to muse on the days of *lang syne* and contrast their pleasing gleams with the darker shades cast o'er the days of closing life—then, active—full of decision and energy—now, languid—indifferent to what is going on in the world, and vexed with trifles. There has been a deplorable change in both the ministers and people within the last forty years. The early inhabitants were more thinly scattered, but they seemed to cling with strong attachment to each other. Ministers were few, but their ministrations were better appreciated than they are now. If their services were inadequately recompensed then, it was from inability, not from indifference to their necessities, as is too much the case now. There was a genial spirit of kindness as well as a warm feeling of nationality in their intercourse with the people, and much more of veneration and respect for their persons—for their office sake—than is paid now, that cheered their toils and animated them in the discharge of their duties, and there was a kindlier spirit of brotherhood among themselves. Then, personal intercourse was seldom, from the immense distances which separated them, but common interests sometimes brought them together for mutual counsel, and whenever the affairs of the Church and the welfare of their respective flocks had been considered, and a course fixed on, there was the relaxation of boyhood — the fun and frolic of youths escaped from the rigour and discipline and the drudgery of hard tasks—enjoyed by men of weightier avocations and graver years; wisdom and wit, humour and folly, happily blended in these intellectual symposiums.

"When I saw you last I promised that you would soon hear from me, but since that time I made a short excursion to Chatham, and now that I am in my private cell I can do no work. In such intolerably hot weather it is a heavy task to wield a *goose's* quill, far more a steel-pen, so that you may expect little of the light and feathery, and much less of the keen and pointed in this epistle. You directed me to a serious perusal of the last page of your last letter—where you speak of a yet untold life—why life! Man, there are not incidents enough to give variety to the annals of an oyster! for I think it was our great Dramatist who has said or hinted that an oyster may be crossed in love. So I will take cooler weather to dip into its fiery mysteries. However, you have set me agoing on a subject which I have long contemplated, namely, to gather together such scraps of interest relating to our Church in Canada as might be useful to some future chronicler of our times.

"I have been in the habit of keeping copies of many of my most

PARENTAGE AND EARLY EDUCATION. 13

important and public letters, and I meant, when I had time, to collect and arrange them, so that if any one some day hence would be at the trouble of reading them they might find something interesting about the affairs of our church. The letters, too, of my clerical correspondents I have kept; but it would take a world of labour to read them and select the useful from such as are on trifling subjects. I regret that I did not take note of passing events; much that would be interesting has passed from my memory, or only recurs now and then as fragmentary dreams, and I may give you a few of the old reminiscences as they come back upon me. You have given texts for a few, and the letters written about the time of Chalmers, Irving, Mary Campbell, and the 'Leetle Verry' on the Rhine, who carried off with her more than a *leetle verry* of my heart, may suggest something more. But, an autobiography! O, no, no; there is neither incident nor public life to make it in the least interesting; nothing to elevate a biography above insignificant gossip. However, as the garrulity of old age when once excited flows on without interruption, I may deluge you yet with a flood of old memories; but, though pleasing to myself, and perhaps to the few remaining who shared the joys of my school-boy days, they can have no interest to another."

To the reader who was not personally acquainted with Dr. Mathieson this may seem rather a dull setting to his ideal picture of a noble, frank, generous and happy nature. But some consideration must be given to the thought that these are the words of one whose years were verging on three-score and ten—whose life had been one of unusual activity—of one, who, tenacious in the last degree of all the rights and privileges, and the respect, appertaining to his *status* as a minister, was loath to concede that the infirmities of age had in any degree incapacitated him for active duties, and whose ardent temperament fretted under such petty vexations and annoyances as are common to humanity and inseparable from old age. During twelve years previous to the date of the above letter he had been aided in the discharge of his pulpit duties by different assistants, and, as time wore on, he gradually became in some measure reconciled to altered relationships which necessity rather than choice had led him in the first place to sanction, but he was ill at ease in the prospect of a more permanent arrangement that was now for the first time proposed, that of the appointment of an assistant and *successor*. He could not brook the idea of any one waiting, as it were, for him to " shuffle off this mortal coil" that he might stand in his vacated shoes. But, do away with any misconception, it is right to mention here that the disquietude of the Doctor's mind at this time was due almost entirely to his own easily excited imagination and the exceeding sensitiveness of his nature, and that the subsequent appointment of an assistant and successor proved on the whole highly satisfactory, not only to the congregation, but to the Doctor himself. We will not further pursue this digression, however, but at once proceed to narrate in his own words the story of his parentage and education, and of the peaceful, happy days that intervened from the time of his leaving college until he received the call and appointment to become the minister of St. Andrew's Church, Montreal.

It may be as well to premise that what follows is made up of extracts from a number of letters, the last of which is dated the the 23rd April, 1866.

PARENTAGE AND EARLY EDUCATION.

"In asking a sketch of my early days you have touched a string that almost spontaneously responds to the slightest excitation. It has been beautifully said, 'there are no remembrances like those of our youth,' and often, within the last few months especially, does my memory revert to my early days. Though they passed away like a delightful dream, and are devoid of incident, to me they are very interesting, and the most trifling occurrences assume the magnitude of the most important events.

"My father was a Highlander, the son of a farmer in Sutherlandshire. His mother died, when he was two or three years old, in giving birth to a daughter. His father married a second time, and, as he alleged, his stepmother was very severe and unkind to him. I have heard him say that often he was sent to the hill to gather in the sheep or feed the cattle amidst the drifting snows, without shoes or stockings on his feet. He longed to see the world beyond the little circle of his native hills. His father became alarmed, and, like Norval's, his anxious care was 'to keep his only son himself at home.' He had learned to read, but his ambition was 'to write and cipher too.' These aspirations increased the old man's terrors, lest he should lose his only son, for every one, he alleged, who could read and write, sought to display their acquirements in 'the low country.' One autumn evening, after feeding the cattle, he requested his father to send him to school, when he received something like the following answer to his request: 'I am just as good a man as you are likely ever to be. You have received as much education as I have. It has served all my purpose—it may do yours. I mean to bring you up in the same profession in which I have lived honestly and respectably

Those who learn to *write and count* get discontented and leave the country, &c.' Whether these resolutions were warmly enforced by his stepmother I do not know, but there was some disagreement which offended him mightily. When all had gone to bed he started for ————, some fifteen or twenty miles off, where a recruiting party were stationed. He accepted the 'Queen's shilling'—and was back by the dawn of the day to the discharge of his domestic duties, without informing any one what he had done, till he was summoned to appear and confirm the deed by being 'attested, sworn and a'. He left amidst the profound grief of his father and only sister, and about three weeks afterwards joined his Regiment—either the 72nd or 78th, I forget which—and in about nine months went with it to the East Indies. He was then about seventeen or eighteen years of age. Under whom he served I do not know. One war had terminated and another was commencing. He remained about seven years without seeing much fighting, when, his health having given way, he was invalided, sent home, and stationed in Dumbarton Castle for garrison duty. Though 'an old fogey,' he was yet a young man, and soon tiring of the indolence and inactivity of garrison duty he became anxious to obtain a discharge and learn some business. His grand-uncle, H. McKay, was barrack-master. He, with sergeant Drysdale, of the artillery, and one or two old men, under the command of Capt. Robertson, constituted the garrison in the renowned fortress. My father's thirst for knowledge was unquenchable. He had learned by this time to write, and now went to a 'night-school,' and became a proficient in arithmetic. He was a prodigious favourite with his commanding officer, and to him he imparted his *high* aspirations of acquiring a scientific knowledge of gardening. Capt. Robertson, however, gave him a letter of introduction to the superintendent of the bleaching establishment at Dalquhurn, and, having visited the print-fields of Cordale and Dalquhurn—then, I believe, the most extensive works of the kind in Scotland—after hesitating for a short time between becoming an engraver, and a copperplate printer, he selected the latter, and was apprenticed to the trade. His commanding officer became his surety and extended to him the privilege of absence from the Castle, excepting 'high days and holidays,' when he appeared in all the pomp and pageantry of military life in the Castle. Upon the breaking out of the French Revolution, in 1792, he had to sleep in the Castle, having to travel every evening after six and to return to Renton before six o'clock next morning—the distance was six or seven miles. Finding it not good to be alone, somewhere about the beginning of the last decade of the eighteenth century he 'courted' my mother, and obtained her consent. But, as the course of 'true love never did run smooth,' *Granny* put a *veto* on their union. She said 'he was a weel-far'd lad, and a' body said he was an unco guid *chiel*, but I dow na bide the ill-far'd name o' a soger.' Her scruples, however, were soon overcome—the *aristocratic* blood of the Rodgers of Cloddach, in matrimonial alliance with the Ewings of Keppoch, submitted to the claims of ardent love, and, to the delight of themselves, and the perfect satisfaction of all parties concerned, George Mathieson and Janet Ewing were united in 'the holy bands of marriage'—forgive me the half Popish phrase—by the Rev. James Oliphant (for whose gifts and graces, see Burns' Holy Fair.) Grandfather was a younger son, or the son of a younger son, of

Ewing of Keppoch, who possessed that estate for about six hundred years, as I have been told, previous to 1816 or 1817, when it passed into the Dunlop family. My mother was born at Roseneath, whence the family removed to the Kirkton of Cardross, that is, the point of land between the Leven and the Clyde. The Kirkton! What myriads of pleasing memories rush on my mind at the very mention of the name. The cottage, with its antique furniture, its beds with wooden shutters for hangings, its boufet and four-legged stools, grandfather's arm-chair in the corner, where sat the venerable man, making 'tow guns' and boats for his numerous 'O's' that constantly frequented his fireside, delighted with his task, and entering with a youthful heart into all their frolics, fun and glee, except when one or two theatrical knights, with chivalric airs, would dare to utter in his hearing, 'My name is Norval;' or, 'Draw and defend thy life,' when they would have to draw off to a respectful distance if they were within reach of his long crutch. But I am diverging from my straight path. My father resided in Renton till about 1803 or 1804. The garrison at Dumbarton was disbanded, and he received a pension of about one shilling and two-pence per day. His family had increased—four sons and four daughters. The three eldest died in childhood. I was the fourth, born on the 1st of October, 1795. All my sisters are still alive (1864). He removed from Renton to Balfron in 1804, and to Campsie, where he lived the remainder of his days, in 1807, where he followed his business as a copperplate printer. Wherever he was he conciliated the affections of his employers. He became an Elder in the parish church of Campsie, and in the discharge of his duties as such frequently associated with the

PARENTAGE AND EARLY EDUCATION.

resident Heritors of the parish, and secured the regard of all of them, who honoured his memory by following his remains to the grave—a respect shown by them to few beneath their own rank. The parish minister, the Rev. Mr. Lapslie, accounted him his right-hand man. Dr. McLeod, his successor, afterwards of St. Columba Church, Glasgow, contracted a friendship with him that continued unabated till the last days of his life, and the recollection of which caused the family to press me to pay a tribute of respect to the memory of the worthy Doctor, by preaching his funeral sermon.(*) Dr. Robert Lee, afterwards the minister of Greyfriar's Church, Edinburgh, and the distinguished professor of Biblical criticism in the University of that city, was also a short time in the parish before my father died. Him he respected as his minister, but I do not think that he cherished, or could cherish, for him the same affectionate esteem as he did for his predecessor, Dr. McLeod. He died in March, if I remember aright, 1845, at the age of eighty-two. My mother survived him ten or twelve years, and died about the age of 93 or 94. When young, she was good-looking, of a remarkably cheerful disposition, and charmed her friends with the

---

(*) The Dr. McLeod referred to was father of the distinguished minister of the Barony Church, Glasgow, Dr. Norman McLeod. In a sermon preached by him shortly after the sorrowful event we find the following allusion to the occasion here referred to.—" The end came at last: It came without any warning. In the middle of the night the cry was heard—low and soft, " Behold the Bridegroom cometh!" It was met by him in Peace. His funeral sermon in Gaelic was preached by his old and valued friend Dr. MacFarlan of Arrochar; and in English by another highly valued friend, the son of his most attached Elder in Campsie, the Rev. Dr. Mathieson of Montreal."

urbanity of her manners and the stories of her early days, which she delighted to repeat. They have passed away. There were few in their station who commanded such universal esteem, or whose memory is more affectionately cherished by numerous surviving friends. 'Uncle George and aunt Jenny,' were household words.

"I was sent to school at Renton, and learned the alphabet under Mr. McKinlay, who afterwards became the rector of the academy at Perth. I believe I learned to read, at least I got credit for being a 'capital speller,' and, being one of four, I think, who were called up at an examination before *the Ministers*, to exhibit our gifts, I beat them all. At length Mr. Slight, the minister of Bonhill, gave me some *kittle* words to spell, which I managed to do, all but one. On my defeat I burst into tears. He consoled me by patting my head and giving me a sixpence, when I imagined I was prodigiously rich. This was the cause of a battle; for one of the competitors told me tauntingly, when I left the school, I had gotten the sixpence for crying, or, because I could not spell the word. Bloody noses and scratched faces were the result, but victory again smiled on me. I commenced Latin with Mr. Hally, of Balfron, but made little progress. I was about a year at a school in Lennoxtown, and afterwards went to the parish school of Campsie, taught by Mr. McFarlane, or 'Liffy' as we called him. Sometimes he was cross and sometimes he was kind, which humours we learned to take advantage of. He had two special favourites, who received a proportionate share of hatred from the others in the school. He was a good man, and we loved and respected him. I think he sent a class of nine to College on the 10th of October, 1809. Some of these failed. Three of them still survive I believe, though of one of them I have not heard for some years—Tom Gordon, into whose insatiable ears I have poured a description of Wallace's sword a thousand times. Happy school-days! light were our cares, transient our sorrows, intense our joys. What dangers we encountered! What toils we endured! Harrying hawks' nests—gimmeling trouts—fighting the boys of other schools. I wish I could enjoy them again, even with their broken heads and bloody noses. But in these penalties I shared little, for, according to the testimony of old Janet Graham, I was "a weel set laddie." I could give you many anecdotes of these school-days, which, however uninteresting to another, have a charm for myself, and no doubt tended to form, in a great measure, the future characters of the actors. But I am not going to philosophize at the end of a chapter. As usual, I have to crave your indulgence for haste and blunders.

Yours, &c.,

A. M.

CHAPTER SECOND.

COLLEGE CAREER AND TUTORSHIP.

We have now come to that interesting period in the Doctor's history when, we must suppose, he made up his mind to qualify himself for a learned profession, for few in his station of life aspired to a college *curriculum* without having that in view. But whether he had at this time in prospect, as the ultimate result of his studies, "to wag his head in a poopit" does not appear, although it is likely that such was the case from the great interest which his father took in church matters and his intimacy with the clergy, by which Alexander would also be brought into frequent contact with them. However that may have been, along with others of Mr. McFarlane's pupils, to Glasgow College he went on the 10th of October, 1809. Like many other Scottish students, the subject of our sketch entered college at an early age. He was then only fourteen, and very small in stature, and, indeed, remained so till about the age that most young men have attained their full height, when, all at once, he shot up to the size of a grenadier. "That was an eventful day"—to resume his own narrative—"when I assumed

the somewhat dilapidated and stained *toga* of my cousin Peter*
who had bequeathed to me his mantle on his entering the Divinity
Hall—my pride being made to humble my vanity by being assured it
was more honourable to sport a *frieze* displaying somewhat of 'skyey
influences' than flaming scarlet. Our Dominie was a proud man
that day when at the head of eight or ten sheepish boys they marched
into the courts of the old College, gazing with wonder at the Lion
and the Unicorn that silently guarded the large broad steps that
seemed the inviting but difficult ascent to the halls of knowledge.
That we might the more easily and gracefully make our bows he
had recommended us to go to the '*dancing school*'—which pre-
cursive polish I contemned—having been denied that privilege a
short time before when I was in the humour to go. Notwithstanding all his maxims of polite and courtly bearing, we huddled together into a corner and stood, ill at ease, on the defensive. At college we wrought hard till the Blackstone Examination † was over:
after that much of our time was spent idly. The second year
little or nothing was done—the far famed battles with the 71st occu-

---

*The late Rev. Peter Napier, of the College Church Glasgow, and
formerly of St. George's-in-the-Fields.

† So called from an old oak chair having a seat of black marble, which
the student under examination occupied. The examination is rather an
initiatory form than a rigid test, and is required of all students before
entering each and all of the gown classes. To the *first year's* student it
is nevertheless sufficiently formidable. The usual first question of the
Professor is, "Mr." so and so—naming him in Latin, "What do *you*
profess?" The general reply being "Doctissime Professor, Evangelium
secundum Joannem Profiteor," when the candidate takes his seat on
the Blackstone and construes a verse or two.

pying the greater part of the winter, and in which the 'Campsies' held a distinguished position. 'Plunking the class,' too, was so frequent as to cause numerous *rows* in 'Jammy's'* class—the absentees on their return being taken for strangers, and the 'strong man' called in to turn the strangers out.

"My father had removed to Woodside on the banks of the Kelvin and there I entered on my labours, at sixteen, as a schoolmaster to the workers at Houldworth's Cotton Mills. My salary was ten shillings per week from the Company, and threepence from each pupil, by which I earned about seven shillings and sixpence per week. It was an evening school. During the day I attended the classes at college, but studied little. In the summer I kept the books and accounts of a cooper who had entered into the herring trade, and received for this my board and 2s. 6d. per week. My pockets were always empty and my coat seedy—but, no help for it but drudge on. Thus passed over about eighteen months during which very little mental progress was made, for which there may be an excuse in the want of time for study, but, what was worse, I lost all habits of application. My good old aunty—a most independent, energetic woman—procured me a tutorship for the ensuing six summer months at Gairlochead, in the family of Captain Campbell, with a salary of five pounds. A few extra pupils brought me about seven pounds more, and, on my twelve pounds, with a suit of clothes from my father, and shirts from my mother, I campaigned the winter, or rather two winters. My pupils made considerable progress, notwithstanding a great deal of broken time—every

---

* James Miller, M. A., Professor of Mathematics.

'sheep-gathering' and 'peat-casting' all hands being required—and in these exercises my health which began to fail me was quite restored. Idly I spent much of my time, but very pleasantly. The afterwards celebrated Mary and Isabella Campbell were my pupils. Isabella was a good creature—amiable and pious. Mary, quick, pretentious, and conceited; she was spoiled by her father, who, proud of her qualifications, exhibited her scholarship on all occasions, and excited in her inordinate vanity and presumption—the foundation of the contemptible fanaticism which afterwards misled Story, Campbell, and Irving. In a word, Mary became a designing hypocrite, or, an arrant fool, which the little education she had, and the natural force of her mental faculties, forbid me to receive. Her cunning and deceit were irrepressible when she was a child, and though my intercourse with her in after life was little, I did not wonder when it culminated in the working of miracles, and in gibbering in 'an unknown tongue.' The extravagances into which her fanaticism led were notorious, and, better that they are buried in oblivion than awaken the pity and disgust of the sober thinking.

"Mary's elocution was good. For a child, she read remarkably well, and her father took every opportunity of exhibiting her gifts. Mr. Robert Campbell of Roseneath had been in this quarter, on business I suppose, and called at Fernicarry. Mary, as was customary, was brought on the stage and dismissed with applause. This led to some expressions of regret from the Captain that I was about to leave them for college, and ended by his recommending me as a tutor to his brother's boys. In the interview which followed I stated my intention not to abandon my college course, but engaged to return as early in spring as possible. This I did, and the next eleven years of my life were spent in Mr. Robert Campbell's family, at the Clachan, in as much happiness as it were befitting mortal to enjoy. It was by far the most eventful period of my existence, if the successes and disappointments of a sensitive and proud spirit could form a marked epoch in mental history. But I must be off to other matters, and I dare say you have got enough *usque ad nauseam* of this for the present."

In these references to his College career there is hardly so much as an allusion to the struggles and privations of student life, but we are not on that account to suppose that *Sandy* Mathieson, as he was called at school, had discovered a royal road to learning. With twelve pounds in his pocket to defray the expenses of a session at college the student, if he *was* clothed in purple, could not hope to "fare sumptuously every day." He would have to be content with a lodgement in the fifth or sixth story of a gloomy "land" of tenements known by such unclassical names as "the Candleriggs," "the Rotten Row," or, "the Cowcaddens." His coat could not be otherwise than "seedy;" and, if there was any virtue in hard beds, he would reap all the benefits thereto belonging. What the Doctor says about the "plunking" * proclivities of his schoolmates and of his own "idle-set" must be taken *cum grano*, for when he left college those who were in a position to pronounce on his acquirements gave unequivocal testimony that he was a young man of extensive learning and of earnest piety.

No student ever better enjoyed a *lark* than did our friend at college. The following may be taken as an illustration of the pranks

---

* *Plunking*, a scotticism for playing the truant.

practised by the "*Colly dongs*"—the soubriquet by which the gowned students were known to the "Keelies."* It will be recognized as a true picture by every who has an experimental knowledge of college life:—"In our anxiety to see Kean the elder, in Macbeth, we were forced by necessity to tempt a douce elder of the Kirk to enter that den of iniquity—a play-house—pretending that we were taking him into a grand Episcopalian Church to hear a *great gun* from London. His free remarks on 'Episcopawlian corruptions'—his amazement and horror when at length he discovered that he was in the *Devil's* house—his subsequent resignation to his fate, when out of the *pit* he could not get—his undoubting conviction of the reality of every thing that passed before his eyes—especially the *witch* scene—and his ultimate gratification with the whole play, would form an admirable chapter in a novel. If it does not already supply the ground work of one of the best scenes in Mansie Waugh, which I am half inclined to believe from the intimacy afterwards contracted between one of our theatrical heroes and Moir, the author of Mansie."

It may be mentioned that the *curriculum* of study at the University, required of a candidate for the ministry, consisted of four years in the "gown classes"—*i. e.* in the Arts, or classical literature department, and four years in the study of Theology, in all its branches, in the Divinity Hall. That was eight years in all; but, by an arrangement at that time permissible—a very bad arrangement—it was allowable for the student to take *partial sessions* in his

* The term "Keelies" was applied to the lower order of Glasgow street Arabs, between whom and the students there has always been waged an interminable warfare.

Divinity course and to extend his studies over an indefinite time. And of this, the Doctor, like many others who with himself were pressed for *the needful* to prosecute an uninterrupted course, availed himself. How long his theological teaching was thus extended we cannot now tell; it is altogether likely, however, that he applied for and obtained license to preach the Gospel as soon as the prescribed term had been fulfilled, and having been licensed to preach in the year 1823—at which time he would be 28 years of age—the presumption may be entertained that it was not until about that time that he had completed the course. At all events, from the time that he began the study of Theology until its consummation a period of full ten years had elapsed, during the whole of which he was living as tutor in the family of Mr. Robert Campbell, of Roseneath, excepting the intervals of his attendance at college.

His first " trial discourse " in the Divinity Hall was to him a *great trial.* For a long time before its delivery he felt no small uneasiness in regard to it. This feeling did not arise from anything like inability to write a sermon, or fear of the professor's criticism, but from the fact that it was then, as it still is, the invariable practice for each theological student to preface the reading of his discourse by the offering up of a brief prayer. Having no faith in his powers of speaking or of praying extempore, and having as little faith in his poor memory, he carefully wrote out a prayer on the back of his manuscript, and for several weeks might have been daily seen perambulating the college green, diligently committing it to memory, till at last he had it at his tongue's end, of which he satisfied himself by repeatedly saying it aloud in the hearing of a congregation of " venerable rooks," whose progenitors had from time immemorial found a home among the branches of a few old trees that stood in a corner of the green, and who were never molested, an old law of the University being yearly read in Latin, prohibiting the students from troubling them.

At last the day of trial comes. The students assemble. Dr. McGill, a distinguished man in his day, takes the chair, and the subject of our sketch tremblingly enters the desk. After a verse or two had been sung, he begins his prayer, fortified by the thought that should memory prove treacherous, and things come to the worst, he could take a quiet peep at his manuscript. After repeating a little of it the thought struck him " What if I should stick ?" the result being utter confusion, or, rather, the mind becoming a perfect blank. In vain he cast his eyes to his paper. Not a word or letter could he distinguish from another, but he managed to stammer a few sentences, which he used afterwards to say must have been " sheer nonsense," and an AMEN. Though terribly crest-fallen he managed to deliver his discourse, and was even complimented by the professor on his first attempt at sermonizing. He was asked to remain at the end of the hour, and accordingly went up to the professor's desk after the class had left, fully expecting a reprimand, but no, the good professor, addressing him, said, " I observed, Sir, that you failed somewhat in prayer this morning, but don't be cast down about that, the very best men in the Church have done the same thing." But for these timely and wise words it is doubtful if he would have further prosecuted his studies for the Holy Ministry, so sensitive was his nature.

Not long after receiving license Mr. Mathieson found himself in " a pulpit "—that acme of ambition for her son of many a good

Scottish dame. It was in the parish Church of Luss, on the banks of Lochlomond, sufficiently removed from Rosencath, as he believed, to obviate the inconvenience of his trying his "prentice hand" at preaching in the presence of friends; but the gardener at the Clachan, who had a great respect for "Maister Alexander," and who, like many others of his class, deemed himself a good judge of sermons, set out in the morning to hear him, and on being interrogated after his return as to how Mr. Mathieson got on, replied, " ou verra weel, Sir—verra weel." "And where was the text ? " continued the questioner; "*a dinna mind that, Sir, but there was a deal about* therefore *in it*." The text being Romans XII, 1. " I beseech you, therefore, brethren by the mercies of God, &c."

In the refined and cultivated society of the inmates of the Clachan and of the neighbouring "gentry" the respect with which the young tutor was at first treated ripened gradually into closest friendship, which neither lapse of time nor distance ever diminished and that were only dissolved by death. Mr. Campbell was the Duke's factor, and Mr. Story informs us that the trait which marked the Clachan family distinctively was their devotion to the house of Argyle, and as an illustration of a highlander's veneration for the head of his clan relates the following amusing instance:—A man came to Mr. Campbell with a long complaint of contumelious usage received at the hands of some adversary or other; " and mair nor that," said he, coming, after a detail of his grievances, to the crisis of his charge, " he had the impiddence to strike me in the pre‗ sence o' *His Grace's Horse !* "

Mr. Drummond was the Minister of Rosencath at the time Mr. Mathieson went to reside in the parish; a man of considerable ability in his day, but at this time quite incapacited from old age for the discharge of public duties.

He was succeeded by the Rev. Robert Story who was an amiable and pious man, and, being young Mathieson's senior by only five years, they came to regard each other with a brotherly affection that never was interrupted until Mr. Story's death in 1859. The Manse was but a short distance from the Clachan, the approach to which was through an avenue over-arched by magnificent yew trees, whose sombre foliage imparted a solemnity—almost a sacredness —to the vicinity, very much in harmony with the poetic tendencies of the tutor's mind. The peninsula and parish of Roseneath lie between the Gairloch and Loch Long, in the estuary of the Clyde, one of the most picturesque spots in all Scotland. "The weariest Pilgrim of the Beautiful could wish to gaze on no lovelier scene." The broad expanse of rippling waters, sea-ward; the sinuous, silent Lochs; the wooded, winding shores; the sparkling roofs and towers of castle and villas rising amongst the trees and gardens, and, towering above all, that majestic chain of rugged rock which from times immemorial has by strange caprice been styled "The Duke of Argyle's Bowling Green." It was amid such scenery that Dr. Mathieson became imbued with that inextinguishable and romantic love for the hills and glens of his native land that so conspicuously characterized him.

CHAPTER THIRD.

RECOLLECTIONS OF DR. CHALMERS AND EDWARD IRVING.

THERE were associations of another kind connected with Mr. Mathieson's sojourn at Roseneath that lingered in his memory as long as he lived. These arose out of the intercourse he then had with two of the most remarkable divines of modern times; the one, in the zenith of his glory; the other, just emerging from comparative obscurity—destined to win his way to unparalleled celebrity. We refer to Dr. Chalmers, and his assistant, the eccentric, but highly gifted Edward Irving—men, both endowed with brilliant and powerful talents, sharing a common inheritance in the domain of genius, yet differing greatly in the tone and character of their eloquence. His recollections of the latter formed the subject of a long and interesting letter, written in 1864, of which the following is the substance :—

"MY DEAR FRIEND,— I have been long in acknowledging your last kind letter, and what excuse have I for my negligence? None! I have had little to do for the last six weeks, and therefore, I suppose, from that natural tendency to do nothing, which some one has declared to be the *summum bonum* of happiness, I determined to be happy. But it would not do. Mental indolence was wretchedness. So, ascending one degree higher in the scale of action, I seized a parcel of old papers and letters which were rotting in a box, and amidst scenes and friends of my early days, I have been holding revelry. Your *phantom* would occasionally intrude and scowl on me for not fulfilling my promise of giving you some personal reminiscences of Edward Irving.

"Irving was a noble-minded fellow, kind, generous, and of a lively genius. But there was one point in his character that I cannot reconcile with true greatness of mind, that is, his excessive vanity. Though he made no pretentious demands on the applauses of others, it was clear that he considered them due to his talents, and when he received them he rolled them as a sweet morsel under his tongue.

"I first met with him at the Manse of Fintry. I think it must have been a very short time before he became assistant to Dr. Chalmers—at that time the minister of St. John's Church, Glasgow. I don't remember what led me to pay a visit of a few days to my old friend Colthard. I was then not licensed to preach, and could give him no relief on Sabbath. So, not to interrupt his preparations, with my fishing rod I repaired to the oft-frequented pool of the Endrick to practice "the gentle craft." It was a Saturday. On returning to the Manse I found that Mr. Irving had arrived, and had already engaged to take the morrow's pulpit duties. He was, from some cause, terribly in the doldrums. He had not succeeded in his expectations, and I think had no employment of any kind, and the future, to his ardent and sensitive

E

mind, presented a picture of unrelieved darkness. In fact, he was not only desponding, he was misanthropical. His finely chiselled face, his dark flowing hair, and the outward squint of his eyes—which somebody has called 'a portentous obliquity of vision'—when his countenance was lighted up with indignation at the want of the world's discrimination, and made gloomy with disappointment, presented him to the imagination as one of those northern demigods whose ire is more to be feared than their love to be courted. I do not remember the character of his preaching on that occasion—there was something peculiar about it—yet it failed to impress me. He formed a thousand projects of future action—was determined to leave his native land and seek for a field of usefulness abroad. Though his purposes were unsettled, and altering every few minutes, he seemed most inclined to proceed on his *own hook*—as the Yankees say—as a Christian missionary to South America. Mr. Colthard tried hard to sooth his mind and give it a more hopeful bent. I remember that I wondered at him, and pitied him—for there was something that, in spite of his eccentricities, commanded respect. On Monday morning he set out to walk across the moor to Glasgow—I do not think there was a public conveyance at that time from Fintry, if there was one from Campsie, which was about half way. But he was strong and resolute, and I am persuaded he would not have availed himself of it. Mr. Colthard and I accompanied him to the top of the hill by 'the Craw Road,' which led across the moor. When we parted from him he threw forward his brawny arms and exclaimed 'farewell! I go—I go—I go. God my guide, the world my field!' and rushed forward on his way. I met with him frequently afterwards, and learned to love him, which I confess I did not do at first. Once, at his earnest invitation, I breakfasted at his lodgings, if I remember well, in Howgate or Charlotte-street. He was engaged on some metaphysi question which absorbed his mind, and though he earnestly tried to be social and conversational, every now and then the subject lagged, and our interview was neither very intellectual nor agreeable. On his 'marriage-trip' he came by Roseneath from the Highlands. I had gone with Mr. Story to visit one of his parishioners who resided in a cottage by the lake side. Looking out from the window we beheld a singular sort of procession—two gentlemen, each bearing on his shoulder a well stuffed carpet-bag, and between the two, a travelling trunk of no ordinary size: following them was a lady, a carpet bag slung over her shoulders and in her hand a large leathern reticule. We speculated with many jokes who these *foreigners* were who had invaded from the north our peaceful parish. On getting home to the Manse the mystery was solved, for we found Mr. Irving, his wife, and Dr. Martin of Kircaldy, his father-in-law. They had come from Inverary, and had crossed Loch Long at Caulport, where they attempted to hire a cart to carry their luggage across the moor. I am sorry to confess the fact, the *good folks* of Roseneath proved as avaricious as their neighbours, and demanded an exhorbitant charge for the service. Indignant at their dishonesty, Irving and his father-in-law determined to shoulder their trunks and proceed a-foot. The evening was spent very pleasantly and they remained over Sabbath, when Dr. Martin preached for Mr. Story. The second evening, immediately after tea, Irving asked me to accompany him on a walk.

"The moon was on the Loch, the evening still and beautiful, and we sauntered along the beach and through the castle woods till it was long past ten o'clock. After a few words of conversation I had no need further to speak. Irving launched forth in a torrent of eloquence, instructing me how I should prosecute my studies, and suit my intercourse with the world. Often afterwards have I regretted that I could not retain in memory his admirable and affectionate instructions, which seemed to flow from the double inspiration of love for his pupil and a deep interest in the cause which prompted his exhortations. I never listened with more interest or delight to so long a lecture—nearly four hours—the sea rolling lazily in upon the beach and the moon in resplendent beauty shining over us."

In another letter, rather long for insertion, we have a graphic description of an excursion to the top of Tamnaharra, the highest point in the parish, in company with Dr. Chalmers, Irving, and a party of ladies. It narrates how Irving carried the ladies in his capacious arms over the sludgy beach to the boat; how he stripped off his coat and vest and rowed the boat alone, a distance of nearly six miles; how, after landing, Irving manifested his *tailoring* powers under the shadow of a great rock, and how, having been suddenly interrupted by his mischievous companions, he fled to the heather, " a souple lad he was and strang "—amidst the roars of laughter which followed him till he was far out of sight; and how, upon another occasion, one of the party assumed the fiddle and Mr. Edward Irving danced a Highland reel on the green, while Dr. Chalmers looked on, rubbing his elbows and clapping his hands in perfect glee.

The Mary and Isabella Campbell above referred to will be readily recognized as chief actors along with Irving and Mr. Campbell, the Minister of Row, in what subsequently came to be known as the Row Heresy. Irving went to London, and no man in the Metropolis was, for a short time, more popular. " But his head got dizzy from the topling height to which he had ascended. He began to put wild meanings on prophecy, to predict the personal advent of Christ, and to speak in unknown tongues." *

Poor Irving was summoned before the Church courts, and deposed, came down to Glasgow, and died there. In the crypt of Glasgow Cathedral was he buried, says Mr. Cunningham, and when the mourners retired they left still standing at his grave a number of young women clothed in white, who confidently expected that he was immediately to rise again. Mr. Campbell was also deposed, and the Row Heresy dwindled away, though the followers of Edward Irving continued for some time to be known as " Irvingites." Subsequently they came to be known as the Catholic Apostolical Church. If our information is correct there are two congregations belonging to this sect in Canada, one in Kingston, and another in Toronto.

We are sorry that the first sheet of the following letter referring to Dr. Chalmers has been mislaid, and we do not recollect its contents further than that allusion was made in it to his first disappointment, no doubt the greatest that he ever experienced. The Parish of Methven, in the Presbytery of Perth, became vacant in November, 1823, by the death of Mr. John Dowe, formerly of Canonbie, who

---

* Cunningham's Church History of Scotland.

had for the long space of forty years discharged the pastoral duties of that parish and taken an active and influential part in the business of the Church courts. It was situated in a beautiful part of the country and was in every respect a most desirable charge. It was one of the old original parishes whose session records went back as far as the Reformation. In 1574, when Mr. James Hering, or Heron, was minister, the following entry appears in the Register of Ministers, out of which it would puzzle a Philadelphia lawyer to construct a hypothesis of the incumbent's stipend : " Mr. James Hering, minister, and now provydit Provoste and Parsone, *per se*, has stipend the twa pairt of his awin Provostrie of Methven, payand the Reidars at Methven and Auldbar, extending to 6 chald., 2 B., 2 pts bier ; 13 chald., 5 B. 3 pts. miel ; and £78.8.5 money. Readar at Methven, with a stipend of £16 and Kirklands." Methven is mentioned in history as early as the year 970, when Colenus, king of the S ots, is said to have been killed in that neighbourhood, and it was in the neighbourhood of Methven castle that the English Army, under the Earl of Pembroke, defeated Robert the Bruce in 1306. This was the parish upon which Mr. Mathieson had set his heart and to aid him in obtaining which he had solicited letters of recommendation from his former preceptor, Dr. McGill, from Principal Macfarlan and *his friend* Dr. Chalmers, " then toiling in the parish of St. John's; charming the city of the west by his exuberant eloquence ; beautifying every topic which he touched ; building churches; founding schools; visiting soup kitchens ; and taking the whole pauper population of the parish under his care." * " When at Glasgow," Dr. Mathieson

---

Cunningham's Church History, Vol. II., pp. 613.

writes, "I thought it my duty to apprise Dr. McGill and the Principal what I had done. The Doctor said he was not likely to be referred to, but if he was, he would be most happy to testify to my conduct and character while in his class. The Principal laughingly said, what do you expect me to say in your favour? Am I to testify that you are an idle fellow—like ' McFarlane's geese'— more fond of your play than your work? Well, well, Col. Smythe is not likely to apply to me; but if he does, if I say nothing good of you, I will say nothing ill.' I had written from Roseneath to Dr. Chalmers, detailing the facts and requesting him as a favour, if he was applied to, to state what he personally knew of me, and that I was aware he had not heard me preach, so that as to ministerial gifts I wished him to say nothing. I had caught a cold. I was in bed fancying myself sick, at least sicker than I was. It was a Saturday afternoon—my boys were out, when the servant brought me the Doctor's reply which ran as follows:—

"'January 2nd, 1824.

"' DEAR SIR:— I can assure you it is not without pain that I decline your request. I feel every disposition to befriend you, but I have made it an invariable rule for a long time to grant no recommendations whatever but on my own independent knowledge. And I do exceedingly regret that I am really not in possession of the requisite data for being the object of a reference upon an occasion in which your interests are so much involved. I fully hope that upon these considerations I shall have the indulgence both of yourself and Mr. Campbell, whose kind hospitality I have the warmest remembrance of. I request my compliments to him, and to Mrs. and Misses Campbell, also to my dear friend, Mr. Story.

I am, Dear Sir,
Yours truly,
(Signed,)   THOMAS CHALMERS.

"Indignant at the tenor of the letter I immediately penned the following reply : —

GLASGOW, January, 1824.

'REV. SIR : — I have received your letter of the 2nd inst. declining to be made an object of reference, except on your own independent knowledge, in a matter in which my interests are involved.

'Had you read my letter carefully, you might have perceived that I asked nothing, if you were referred to, but what you could state from your personal knowledge. In making my request I conceived I was demanding a privilege, rather than asking a favour, though I couched my solicitation in the more obsequious form. The " young scions " of the Church naturally, and in my opinion, rightfully, look to their superiors for advice and guidance, and for the many kind counsels I have received from you I sincerely thank you ; but I think also they have a right to look for such encouragement and support from their superiors in office as the extension of their patronage might bestow, at least in so far as moral character and literary attainments might warrant.

'But you say you do not know me. It is now some two or three years since that on a Saturday afternoon you walked across the Moors from Glenfinnart to the Manseof Roseneath. Mr. Story was from home, but, should any stranger arrive at any time in his absence, he had requested me to attend to their comfort; accordingly I made myself known to you and invited you to the Clachan, where I assured you, you would meet a kind reception. I introduced you to Mr. Campbell and his family, and you were induced to remain with them till Monday. During our intercourse these two days, independently of the testimony of the family, I think you might have personally known something of me. Next summer, I think it was, you came on a visit to Mr. Smith of Jordan hill. At his hospitable table I oftener than once met with you; but, what was more to the point, you requested that as often as I could, I should call on you, and guide you to the most interesting and picturesque points of view in the neighbourhood. This I did. I profited by our walks. I thank you for the counsels you gave me. Our intercourse, though I was not gifted with conversational powers, seemed to be pleasing. During that time, if you did not know me, I think you should have known something of me.

'The following winter, I went to Glasgow to complete my studies, when I had the honour of breakfasting with you twice, and dining once, and, at your request taught one of your Sunday schools, and on the first Monday of every month was with you and your Sabbath-school teachers when they assembled to report progress. In these interviews, if you did not know me, I think you ought to have known me. Afterwards, when you with your family resided for three months at Ardincaple Inn, I had frequent opportunities of meeting with you on occasions both of serious intercourse and healthful amusement, when both character and acquirements had an opportunity of being displayed. If you did not know me then, I think you ought to have known me.

F

'You have not heard me preach. This I mentioned in my letter and said I did not wish you to say anything about my qualifications as a preacher, but that you should simply state what from your own personal knowledge you knew of me, and, I think you ought to have known something. Since I sent off my letter to you I have been informed that you have recommended another to Col. Smythe as a fit person to fill the vacant charge at Methven. Had you stated this as a reason for declining my request I might have admired your candour and consistency, but, since you did not, I may mention, and I am persuaded my information is correct, you could not have recommended *him* on your personal knowledge; for you had never seen him until a very short time before you brought him under Col. Smythe's notice. You had heard him preach one sermon, and at the solicitation of a friend you wrote to Col. Smythe strongly recommending him—of course on " your own independent knowledge" of his *one* sermon.

'This I admit you do not know, namely, to which side of Church politics I belong. This I do not intend to make known to you, or to any one else, until I see a fit time for making the discovery; but, in asking you the favour I did, don't think that I mean to make your mighty name a stepping stone into office, or to bring myself into notice by your flattering commendations, even were they granted. That I would scorn to do, even in a less sacred matter than that which has called forth these remarks.

'But I beg your pardon, though you had many opportunities of knowing something of me in other respects, I must confess you are ignorant of the spirit with which I would contemn everything like sycophancy, or mounting to notoriety on the shoulders of another.

I am, Rev. Sir,
Your most obedient servant,
ALEXANDER MATHIESON.'

" This reply terminated all friendly intercourse with the Doctor, who in writing to Mr. Story some time afterwards seemed tickled with some of the phrases employed and desired him to ' allay my dirdum.' Some years afterwards, walking down Leith walk with the late Doctor Boyd of the Edinburgh High School, we again met. Boyd stopped and conversed with the Doctor, I bowed and passed on; he asked Boyd who I was, said he knew me well when brought to his recollection, and wondered I had not stopped to speak to him ; to which I replied, ' the Doctor only knows me when it pleases him ; I only know the Doctor when it pleases me.'

" It was not till 1837 that I again saw him. I was commissioned by the Synod or a Committee of the Church to put myself in communication with him in relation to our Clergy Reserve's question. I had gone with Principal McFarlan to London on the matter; saw Mr. Morris just before his return to Canada, and learned from him the state in which the question stood. There was much still to do. Doctor Chalmers was then in London, lecturing on his favourite topic. I called at his lodgings repeatedly but never found him at home. At length I made myself known to Mr. Collins, his satellite, and communicated my message, requesting him to lay it before the Doctor. At last a time and place were fixed for an interview, but so large a party had assembled to meet with him, some on business, and others to gratify their curiosity, that I had to wait a long time

A good many I found had been very unceremoniously greeted, and the general plea was used that he had come to London for a special purpose which occupied his whole time. When I came forward, the same excuse of want of time to attend to anything else than the matter in hand was given. I stated that I had executed my commission as I best could, and had only to report to those who employed me what had been done. He requested me to call upon him in Edinburgh when he would give full attention to our business, while I urged the importance of his using his influence in London, where it would have much more effect. It was in vain; he was full of the benefits arising from the parochial scheme and strongly in favour of a friendly coalition with the English Church. He was not decided as to the advantages to be derived from a union of Presbyterians, so wedded were seceders to dissent; to introduce them into the Church would ultimately, he thought, destroy the success of his theory. I got an audience of nearly an hour, but it was quite fruitless, for the whole of the time was occupied by an enthusiastic rhapsody on the Parochial scheme. At length taking my hand, he said my face was familiar to him, he must have seen me somewhere. I replied that about fifteen years ago I had met him at Roseneath. This seemed to bring back a flood of recollections, but he again excused himself for not attending to the Clergy Reserves measures, and so we parted, and, for ever, in this world.

"You will see from this meagre sketch that a distinguishing peculiarity of the Doctor's mind was a complete surrender to the subject occupying his attention, and that he seemed to be more of a partizan than in reality he was; every thing gave way to the idea that engrossed his mind at the time and imparted that inconsistency to his conduct that too frequently marked it. Perhaps, too, you may descry something of that obstinacy and impatience in the above correspondence which has oftener than once displayed itself in the conduct of your correspondent."

The impression made on this writer's mind by the above correspondence tended to lower very much his estimate of the character of the renowned Scottish preacher. His conduct appeared on this occasion to be cold and heartless, and in our reply to Dr. Mathieson we had hinted or said, "a fig for such friendship." This drew from him the following apology for Dr. Chalmers, which is worthy of preservation as evidencing a fine forgiving spirit and conveying also good advice to such as are prone to jump at conclusions:

"I would be very sorry indeed, if my letter to you of May last has in any way disturbed the ideal you had formed of the amiable and child-like Dr. Chalmers. There is a feeling of disappointment when the notions we have formed of the figure, the manners, or habits of any distinguished man are shaken or driven to the winds that is absolutely unbearable. A thousand beautiful visions are dispelled, a thousand irreconcilable facts quite perplex us, the unity of our hero is lost, and instead of the unique individual which our fancy had pictured we have presented a motley figure of the most contradictory proportions. It is human to be composed of mixed ingredients. No man is all sinful or all holy —all morally base, or all morally good. When the grand characteristic features impress our minds we will allow nothing to interfere with our ideal; the shades which soften and beautify the picture are kept out; we are dazzled by the brilliancy of the object. The Doctor was truly a man of unaffected simplicity. His little knowledge of the business of life, and the absorption of his mind by scientific or literary pursuits, made him, in the estimation of the vulgar public, more than eccentric. He was known, as I understand, by the general soubriquet of 'Daft Tammy Chalmers', but there was a genuine simplicity about him which in *your* idea of him I would not have you forget. It was when he was forced into public life that his enthusiasm led him into incongruities of conduct, and he did not judge of matters as others of more worldly views would have done.

Yours very truly,

A. M."

CHAPTER FOURTH.

APPOINTMENT TO ST. ANDREW'S CHURCH. HIS ORDINATION AND ARRIVAL IN CANADA.

Mr. THOMAS Clark, afterwards D.D., was the successful candidate for the Parish of Methven, and continued to be the minister of it, and a leading member of the Presbytery, till 1841, when he was translated to Edinburgh. He was for many years the zealous and efficient Convener of the Colonial Committee of the General Assembly. To Mr. Mathieson the disappointment was such as his sanguine temperament ill fitted him to bear with equanimity, and it would even seem that it gave rise to serious intentions of abandoning his profession for the practice of medicine, this bent having probably been given to his mind by a previous attendance upon a Course of Lectures on Anatomy. That his heart was still in the ministry, however, is evident from a memorandum written by him at Roseneath on the 1st October, 1826: "This day I enter on my thirtieth year, and I trust on the most useful portion of my life. If it shall please God to spare me in the land of the living till a good old age, half that period has already elapsed, and with it have passed away, unimproved, many opportunities which I enjoyed of fitting myself more perfectly for the business of this world, and of preparing myself for the next. Many serious reflections, many bitter regrets, is the anniversary of my birth calculated to awaken. May they come with firmer resolutions of being more active for the future. The prospect of a wider sphere of usefulness opens before me, and may God prepare me to discharge my duties with dispositions and energy becoming their great importance. The profession which I have made choice of from my earliest recollection, while it is the most honourable in this world, is also the most awfully responsible. May God ever preserve a just sense of these truths in my mind, that I may neither bring disgrace on the heavenly religion which He has called me to proclaim, nor endanger my own soul by trifling with the souls of other..........Something like reproach occasionally steals across my mind that I should leave a family where I have been so honoured and so tenderly treated at a time when perhaps my services were most required. But I have the satisfaction to think that my dear boys are likely to do honour to themselves and to reflect credit on all concerned with them by their conduct as scholars and gentlemen.............A few days more, and I must bid the heathery hills of bonnie Scotland adieu. I will be far o'er the sea, and among a people I know not, casting a wistful remembrance to the friends and scenes I left behind me. Pleasing recollections from the long catalogue which shall soothe a sad moment in a distant land!"

The sphere of usefulness here referred to was the charge of St. Andrew's Church and congregation in Montreal, to which he at this time received the appointment. Although he had considerable interest with the Argyle family and also with the Earl of Montrose, besides the patronage of the Principal of Edinburgh College and Principal McFarlan of Glasgow, who ever proved to him a staunch and steady friend, Dr. Mathieson records his satisfaction that he was indebted particularly to no one for this appointment, " The duties of which I will endeavour to discharge with fidelity and zeal, and if I ever return to my native land I will be the better prepared for the service I will be called to. I hope I shall return for my poor father's sake who feels very much at the prospect of my departure. At all events in two or three years I hope to revisit Scotland, and perhaps to get a wife. *I will be marriageable by that time.*" This was a subject that seems to have presented itself to his mind at sundry times, and in diverse manners. He was an ardent admirer of the fair sex, though that admiration was manifested in a general rather than a particular manner, which proved a barrier to the consummation of his wishes in this regard and postponed the " happy day" for many years. He had accustomed himself to regard the matter from a philosophical point of view, and as one and another fair friend receded from his view he consoled himself that there remained as good fish in the sea as ever came out of it. And besides, he had very exalted ideas of the marriage state. "If I could bring myself to look on matrimony," he wrote, " as a matter of mere worldly convenience and comfort, I would be less scrupulous, but my wife must be my companion, my friend, one who is truly pious, and who will lead my soul with her own, morning and evening, to the throne of our Maker. I by no means expect to find a perfect being, nor would I wish it, but one whose imperfections would be so brightened by her virtues and piety that we would bear one another's burdens and participate in one another's joy."

Apprehensive that in the opinion of the *profanum vulgus* he might soon be branded as a *sticket* minister, and morbidly brooding over his recent disappointment, the rejected candidate for Methven was one day walking disconsolately down the side of the Clyde in the neighbourhood of Govan, when a friend and relative, one of the Napiers, met him. Napier saw at a glance that something was wrong, and enquired what was the matter. Mr. Mathieson disclosed the thoughts that were then rankling in his breast, and indicated very plainly that if he thought he could succeed in business he would abandon the ministry. His friend advised him to cheer up and not to do any thing rashly, adding, that, should he finally determine to go into business, he would find a situation for him. Napier asked him to return with him to Glasgow, which he did. In Glasgow they went into an "eating house" to get some refreshment. While sitting there in a room by themselves the door was opened by a gentleman in whom Napier at once recognized a friend from Montreal. Being invited to join them, the conversation turned upon the occasion of this gentleman's visit to Scotland. Having stated his business Napier asked him if he had nothing else in view. "Yes," said he, "I have; St. Andrew's Church in Montreal, to which I belong, is vacant, and the congregation deputed me, when coming to Scotland, to make inquiries for a minister." "*There's your man,*" said Napier, pointing to Mathieson. The latter, being asked as to his willingness to accept the charge, did not long hesitate in expressing it. After some consultation with Mr. Burns, the former minister of St. Andrew's Church and who was specially charged with the selection of his successor, the result was, Mr. Mathieson's appointment and departure for Canada.

At the Synod of Glasgow and Ayr, which met on the second Tuesday of October, 1826, application was made by the Presbytery of Dumbarton for leave to meet on the 19th of that month, in advance of the regular meeting, for the purpose of proceeding to Mr. Mathieson's ordination, and expediting his departure Canada. The petition was unanimously granted, and on that day the Presbytery met accordingly and in due form he was "set apart" for the Holy Ministry. And the Doctor has been heard to refer with lively satisfaction to the fact that a large number of "the brethren" from the Glasgow Presbytery graced the occasion with their presence in testimony of respect and esteem for him, as well as to manifest their disapprobation of "the remonstrance" * which had been sent to that Presbytery from Canada.

If any particular account of the solemn ordination services was preserved, we have not been able to lay hands on it; and therefore suppose that the proceedings were conducted in a satisfactory manner to all concerned. We may be sure that "the imposition of hands" was not forgotten, for that was a part of the ceremony for

---

* "There had arisen some coolness between the congregation of St. Gabriel-street and St. Andrew's in consequence of a communication secretly concocted and sent to almost every Presbytery in Scotland. It was termed *a remonstrance*—setting forth that the then ministers of St. Gabriel's had offered their services to the congregation of St. Andrew's Church: that they were dissenters, disaffected to the Church of Scotland: that there was sufficient clerical strength for the dispensation of ordinances to both congregations: that they had not fulfilled their obligations to former

which the Doctor was a great stickler, and concerning which there is a good story told by Galt, in his "Annals of the Parish," which the Doctor used to relish greatly. Although Mr. Galt makes the anecdote suit the creation of his own fancy, the real hero of the story was the then eccentric Minister of Govan, Mr. Thom, who being present at an ordination could not, for the press, get near enough the candidate to place his hands upon his head, but, instead, reached forth a ponderous staff, which he carried, and touching the young man's head with it remarked in audible, if not very complimentary, tones,—"*timmer to timmer—this must do for the present.*" That the inevitable Presbytery *denner* took place does not admit of a doubt, for, otherwise, in those days the work would not have been accounted "half done." The following reference to a Presbytery dinner may or may not apply to the date of his ordination but is sufficiently apropos to the occasion: "I must tell you how Dr. G. spoiled a fine speech I was making with his dry jokes. I was going on, I believe, making the most strong protestation, that in whatever quarter of the world I might wander, there was *one* old lady I would never forget, and whose health I meant to propose. The light of beauty might grow dim, and th smile of love cease to stir my breast, but the kindness of my old

---

incumbents, &c., &c., and therefore cautioning Presbyteries not to send another minister to Montreal. When the nature of the document became known to Mr. Burns he became very indignant, drew up a reply and sent copies to several Presbyteries. But the selfish spirit of the document itself was a sufficient answer, and but little notice was taken of it. This matter, however, caused a bitterness of feeling to exist between the two congregations, which was not removed for years afterwards.

APPOINTMENT, ORDINATION AND ARRIVAL IN CANADA. 53

friend.—'Wha ist?' said the Doctor; 'is it auld Lady B——? I see y're no gaun to wander through the warld yet, gin ye can wile the auld lady wi your winsome speeches into matrimony. There is ae thing: ye'll no be fashed wi mony bairns.' The whole table were in an uproar. I said I was going to propose the health o' her bairns too, and may she aye boast 'o as mony soucy chiels as I see around me. My toast is, ' *The auld wife 'o Dumbarton and her bairns.*' The joke was unforseen, and the good Doctor quaffed to the auld wife with all his heart. The joke is this—a young scion of the Kirk—and you know they are extraordinarily *blate* in general—being called upon for a toast declared he had none. One of the members present said to him 'give us a young girl then!' 'I hae nane tae gie,' was the reply. 'Surely you can give us an auld wife then.' 'Weel, I'll gie ye the Presbytery of———' The joke was good, and from that time the Presbytery denominates herself ' the auld wife.' "

Before leaving Scotland he made a parting pilgrimage of the Presbytery of Dumbarton and received so much kindness and so many expressions of earnest hopes for his future happiness and usefulness as lead him to say " it melted my very heart into a jelly !" He visited Paisley and preached for his intimate friend the Rev. Patrick Brewster of the Abbey Church. " After sermon," he says, " a military gentleman waited on me to present me with *ten shillings,* being the pay of the officiating chaplain for the day. (The yeomanry cavalry were on permanent duty, and attended divine service.) In vain I protested I had nothing to do with the money—the unknown insisted I should take it, and there was no contending the point, for a priest would have no chance with a soldier in braudishing steel—unless it was in the bloodless shape of a pen. What shall I do with my ten shillings? Being the first money I have received for preaching, I am proud of it—it is from the King.— I think I shall buy a purse with it to hold my savings, and then I am sure it will be a lasting memento, as it is never likely to be the worse for the wear."

At last the day of his departure from the Clachan and from auld Scotia came. "There was a singular melancholy this morning in our little parlour. Breakfast passed in silence. My baggage had been sent off early by the steamer under charge of a servant, while I was determined to linger as long as I possibly could on 'the sweet Isle of the blessed.' I went to the kitchen to bid farewell to the servants. The kitchen is often a *melting* scene, and was particularly so now in another sense. I pretended to laugh at the tears of the poor girls, but my heart was sad. I was a particular favourite of the old nurse and permitted her liberty of speech, which I was always very cautious in allowing to the other servants, and of this she was not a little proud, she, supposing that she might extend her prerogative at the moment of separation, clung round my neck and poured out a torrent of tears. Then came my "Aunty Betty," who had been evidently mustering courage to meet this moment. The half smile with which she met me vanished like the dew-drop in the sun when she attempted to speak. 'O Math'son we have had our quarrels—they were never deadly ones—the sun never went down on our wrath—and now my heart is breaking to part with you. Go, go, and God's blessing be with you, when you return your poor old Aunty Betty will be laid in the dust;' and with that she sprung to her room, and I left that sweet abode of my purest and happiest days with feelings I would in vain try to describe. It was something of a wild vacuity of mind that was almost insensible to all that was passing around."

But the ordeal of parting with the members of the family, with the friends at the manse, and, last of all, with his good old father, was a scene "utterly overwhelming," and too sacred to be described. It was evening when he got aboard the steamer for Liverpool, and, being thoroughly exhausted with the anxieties of the day he retired to his cabin and found some relief in a flood of tears. " You will laugh at my weakness. I care not I would rather be ridiculed than be without feeling : if it has its pains it has its pleasures." Next morning he was tumbling amid the meeting of waters, off the Mull of Cantyre, in a very subdued state of mind, taking a last look at Caledonia's " rugged strand " and pensively muttering to himself " Fare-well, fare-well; my native land ! " &c. A few days were spent " pleasantly enough " in Liverpool till the 16th November, when he found himself on ship-board, bound for New-York. It was a moment of "mingled agony and delight." The ship was just getting under weigh, and there stood on the quay a little knot of friends waving adieu. "I kept my eye fixed on them as long as I could distinguish them among the crowd, and then I felt as though I were an outcast on the world, and abandoned myself to the luxury of grief, while the good ship, under a crowd of sail, was soon in the 'Fair way' of the English Channel. During the night the wind increased greatly, and when I awoke it blew very fresh and the ship was pitching furiously. I attempted to get up; but not having been yet long enough on board to keep the centre of gravity I was pitched headlong on the floor of my cabin, became very sick and made the best of my way to bed. When at length I got on deck, I found that my fellow-passengers had all been *prodigiously* sick with the exception of one, a very fat man, who went about wringing his hands and asking the sailors if they were afraid, and to augment his horrors the fellows told him it was impossible that the ship could outlive the gale another hour. The wind blew furiously. The sails were close-reefed, and we were careering through the water at the rate of twelve knots an hour. The sea was awfully grand, and there was something overpowering in the idea of solitude so complete."

Cape Clear was passed the next morning, by noon they were out of soundings, and, with studding-sails set, they were soon on the bosom of the broad and boisterous Atlantic. On the 3rd of December they were overtaken by a storm. "Towards evening the wind became exceedingly tempestuous, and whatever was not firmly lashed down was rolled about with great violence. Most of us had retired to our *cribs* earlier than usual. Though the noise of the waves breaking against the sides of the ship, the gurgling murmurs of their broken strength, the moaning of the wind through the cordage, and incessant creaking of the timbers, formed no sweet lullaby, still, I slept very soundly till midnight when the captain called us on deck to observe two *ignes fatui* that flitted along the yard-arms of the mizen and main-top masts. This appearance is by sailors accounted ominous, and combined with the gloom of the night was certainly adapted to strike terror into every heart not well fortified against superstitious fears. The swell of the sea was awfully grand. The tops of every wave seemed a sheet of pale fire, a striking contrast to the long dark, hollow troughs between, into which every few moments the ship plunged as if seeking destruction. The gale increased until mid-day following when the sight became truly sublime. I would not have lost the spectacle which the furious, foaming sea then presented for whole months of summer sailing. The huge billows like dark green mountains, their tops of purest white, interspersed with emerald tints, rolled fearfully along. Now they hung their immense mass of water almost perpendicularly over us, threatening us with instant destruction, and then, as the ship rose buoyant on their surface, they went whizzing past, as if murmuring that they had been disappointed of their prey. The fat man's alarm increased with the gale, and, before it abated, he had written his 'last will and testament' and put it into a sealed bottle ready to be hove over board."

Without further incident worthy of note they reached their desired haven and cast anchor inside of " Sandy Hook " on the 13th of December, having made what was then accounted a rapid passage of twenty-seven days. We will not here detail Mr. Mathieson's first impression of America, though they are before us in terse and vigourous words: suffice it to say that he soon discovered for himself those salient points of American character that float on the surface of society, and which European writers usually seize upon with avidity. He thought Broadway was " rather a handsome street, with some neat buildings, chiefly of brick," from which, however, his attention was now and then attracted by the eccentric dress of some of the females, as well as of some of the male gender. " Generally speaking the ladies are not handsome ; they are not trim about the ankles: they want the fine swell and expansion below the waist of an English lady, and their busts are shockingly bad ; they want the bloom and expression of mingled simplicity and archness which distinguish our Scotch lassie, but still their countenances are rather pretty, and some of them have beautiful black eyes." But he ascertained that the ladies were in general far more intelligent, and their information more extensive, than the male sex, and that they could talk politics, and even knotty points of theology, with the greatest facility. He was surprised at the gastronomic feats performed by his fellow-lodgers in the City Hotel, and took note of their chewing and smoking proclivities with *the usual accompaniments.* On the Sabbath morning he worshipped in the Scotch Church and heard an excellent Calvinistic discourse from a Mr. Philips. In the afternoon he attended service in the Episcopal Church where he heard a good sermon and was charmed with the music. In the evening he stepped into one that he saw lighted up, and which proved to be a Universalist meeting-house. It was crowded to excess, " but, such silly trash was never pronounced from human lips as came from him who professed to teach the auditory."

After a week's sojourn in New York he arrived in Montreal, on Christmas eve, where he met with a kind reception from his people and the Protestant community in general, and on the following Sabbath was introduced to his new charge by the Rev. Archibald Connell of Martintown.

He had come out with a small stock of sermons which were soon exhausted, and this caused him to work hard and to draw largely on the hours of the night. However, he wrought cheerfully, visited frequently, reserved a large portion of time for pleasant recreation, and, as the labour became by habit lighter, he gradually became reconciled to the " banishment " from home. But ere three years had elapsed he began to long for a sight of his native land, and to breathe once more his native air. He went "home," and was afterwards heard to say that, had he not done so, *he must have died.* Love of country was with him a passion. He found his friends in Scotland little altered from what he left them, and returned to Canada in good spirits, thoroughly cured for the time being of his home sickness. His congregation steadily increased, and amid new friends and new attachments the feeling of separation wore off and, save in his more pensive moods, his deep-rooted love for the "land of brown heath and shaggy wood" assumed a cheerful and romantic cast.

Shortly after coming to Canada his sensitive mind was sadly shocked by an occurrence of a very tragic kind, and which rendered it peculiarly difficult for him to bring his mind, for some time afterwards, to bear closely upon any subject. Seated in the house of his friend Mr. Robert Watson, the flour inspector, and in social conversation with him, he was suddenly startled by the report of a pistol which had been fired through the window by an assassin with deadly aim. Mr. Watson was fatally wounded and survived only till the following evening. "I shall never forget," he remarks in his funeral sermon, " the innocent, the interesting conversation that preceded that awful moment when the thunders of the cowardly, cold-blooded assassin so suddenly interrupted the tranquillity of our domestic repose ; and introduced death, and lamentation, and woe—literally in the manner expressed in our text— ' for death hath come up into our windows,' (Jeremiah ix., 21.) among those who, but a moment before, felt perfectly secure from harm, and happy in each other's society." The motive which instigated the crime, and the perpetrator of it, both remain to the present day in the profoundest mystery. The sermon alluded to was preached on the 8th April, 1827, and was published at the request of the congregation. Apart from the melancholy interest attached to the occasion of its delivery, it was worthy of preservation as the preacher's first attempt at authorship. He had never before seen himself in print, and it was not till after he had been repeatedly solicited, by friends whom he did not wish to disoblige, that he at last consented to surrender his manuscript.

Mr. Mathieson soon discovered that a very different ecclesiasticism prevailed in Canada from that which he had left behind him in the Presbytery of Dumbarton. There, in every matter of dispute or difficulty that arose, recourse was had "to the law and the testimony." Here, every Kirk session was a law to itself, for neither Presbytery nor Synod existed whose jurisdiction was acknowledged by the few and widely separated ministers of the Church of Scotland. Besides himself, there were but five Kirk ministers in all Canada in active work; these were Dr. Harkness of Quebec, Messrs. Henry Esson and his colleague Edward Black, of St. Gabriel-street Church, Montreal, John McKenzie of Williamstown, and Archibald Connell of Martintown. Mr. Sommerville and Mr. Easton, the former ministers of St. Gabriel's and St. Andrew's, though both residing in Montreal, had retired from ministerial work. It is true there were a few other Presbyterian ministers—chiefly ministers of the Associate Church of Scotland, or "Seceders," who had constituted themselves "the United Presbytery of Upper Canada." In course of time, "the United Synod" was formed and continued its meetings until 1840,

APPOINTMENT, ORDINATION AND ARRIVAL IN CANADA. 61

when its members, to the number of eighteen, were received into connection with the Synod of the Church of Scotland in Canada, but, from these, the Kirk ministers above named had previously stood aloof in the attitude of a "dignified neutrality," conforming their procedures, as best as they could, to the polity set forth in Pardovan, Cook's Styles, or Hill's Practice. How long they would have remained in this isolated condition, if they had been left to themselves, it is impossible to conjecture. And it must be regarded as an anomaly in religious jurisprudence that the propriety of forming Presbyteries and Synods of our Church in Canada was first suggested by the "Civil Magistrate." In the very earliest records of the Synod we find that a certain number of ministers and commissioners from the congregations in connection with the Church of Scotland in Canada met pursuant to agreement in the church of Kingston on the 7th day of June, 1831, when Mr. McGill, in explanation of the object of the meeting, called the attention of members to Sir. George Murray's despatch to Sir John Colborne, Lieutenant Governor of Upper Canada, "relative to a union between the different classes of Presbyterians, to the necessity of forming Presbyteries and a Synod in Canada; and of applying to the General Assembly for recognition."* After "long deliberation" on these points a unanimous decision was arrived at, and, on the following day, the Synod of the Presbyterian Church in connection with the Church of Scotland met for the first time, and was constituted with prayer by its moderator, the

---

* The inconvenience of dealing with individual ministers in relation to Clergy Reserves doubtless suggested the recommendation of the government at that particular time.

Rev. John McKenzie. The number of ministers who were present at these deliberations was fourteen. Of this number there are only three now living. Dr. Urquhart of Cornwall—the only surviving Minister in Canada who was then present—Dr. Cruickshank, formerly of Bytown, now the minister of Turriff, Scotland, and the Rev. T. C. Wilson, formerly of Perth, and now of Dunkeld, Scotland. The story of the Kirk in Canada, prior to the time of Mr. Mathieson's arrival, is bound up in the biographies of a very few individual ministers; and its subsequent history must be sought for elsewhere than in these pages. It has had its seasons of trial and depression. It has figured on the arena of controversy. It has stood on the defensive and shewn a bold front to a powerful rival, and it has been torn and divided by that distinctive attribute of Presbyterianism that delights in "Testimony Bearing." But, it can recount, too, its "times of refreshing," and, we make bold to say, not boastfully, but in a thankful spirit, that it has throughout maintained a consistent and honourable position in the land, and that its prospects now are brighter than at any period in its history. There are now on the Synod's Roll one hundred and thirty-two ministers, and that number falls far short of indicating the growth of Presbyterianism; for, from the division that occurred in 1844, there has sprung up a vigourous Church with two hundred and ninety-five ministers, making in all four hundred and twenty-seven ministers of the Presbyterian order in the Provinces of Quebec and Ontario alone—known by the name of the Canada Presbyterian Church—to which, if we add the numbers in the Lower Provinces, it will probably appear that the Presbyterian element outnumbers all other denominations in the Dominion. And we greatly misapprehend the signs of the times if a general union of these churches is not consummated before long, without waiting for the mandate of His Excellency, the Governor General. It were an insult, however, to Dr. Mathieson's memory did we lead the reader to infer that such a consummation would have been agreeable to his feelings. He never could bring himself to coincide with the opinions of those who advocated a general union of all the Presbyterian Churches as a matter of expediency—or, upon the ground that a numerically large church must necessarily exercise a correspondingly extensive influence on public morals. In fact he deprecated every proposal that was based on such principles, and, in terms so strong as to give colour to the impression that he was opposed to union on any terms. But such was not the case, as we shall by and by endeavour to shew.

CHAPTER FIFTH.

1831.

VISIT TO SCOTLAND AND THE CONTINENT. DISAPPOINTMENTS AND VISIONARY PLANS. HIS MARRIAGE. DEATH OF HIS CHILD.

THIS date opens up a new era in Mr. Mathieson's history, when he took his place as an influential member of the church courts now established in Canada. But, that we may not lose sight of the individual in the crowded and sometimes stormy arena of debate, it will be better to continue our domestic annals, even though it will compel us, in a succeeding chapter, to return to this point. As there is no evidence to the contrary, we suppose that for some time after his return from Scotland he took heartily with his work, and that St. Andrew's congregation continued to prosper under his ministry; that everything, in short, went with him as quietly and satisfactorily as he could reasonably wish or expect. Of this, indeed, we feel assured, for we find this entry in his journal, under date the 17th of March, 1834: " There is some talk of my being promoted to Quebec; however, that is very questionable. I have not made application for the vacant church there, nor will I do so,

Many others have. The salary is a little better, being nearly £500 per annum; however, I think my own will, ere many years, be nearly as good, *and I have a kind flock.*"

Further on we read: "Two months ago I asked one year's leave of absence from my people, and had a quiet refusal, on the ground that no other individual would suit them so well as myself. This was flattering enough, *but not satisfactory.*" He had been unwell, perhaps he again had had a touch of home-sickness; perhaps he was "heart-sick." We cannot now enter upon a diagnosis of his malady, and it matters not. In 1836 he was again *hors du combat,* and allusion to his shaven crown leads us, in this instance, to infer that weariness of the flesh had been induced by "overmuch study." It does not seem, however, to have impaired his relish for the humourous—a very marked trait in his character, and one that he may almost be said to have carried with him to the grave. It is rare to meet such unexceptional pleasantry, and it is well that it should be duly appreciated. That others appreciated this quality in him appears in the following extract from a letter written by an Episcopalian gentleman, one who is no mean judge of men and things, shortly after the Doctor's death : "Though I knew the 'old Doctor' less intimately than I should like to have done, I was sufficiently acquainted with him to have acquired a very sincere regard for him. It was pleasant to meet him, for religion was brightly reflected in the cheerfulness of his character. Moreover, he belonged to a type of our race that is becoming uncommon and bids fair to become extinct. He was natural, genial, and courteous. There was a hearty raciness about him that became contagious, and people found themselves happier for meeting one who seemed to be the very embodiment of happiness and contentment. I often speak of him as an example of christian cheerfulness thoroughly worthy of imitation." But here is the good Doctor's own reference to what was no doubt a severe illness: "I told you that I had been unwell. I am once more myself again, though I had rather a hard time of it for two or three days, and I look now like a renovated being in a nice new wig, the doctor, cruel fellow, having insisted that I should part with my gray birses. I am not quite up to the management of the concern yet, for last Sabbath morning, going into church, off went my cap, and in it the wig, and forward I marched, all the while unconscious I was exhibiting my shaven pole to the staring eyes of many beholders, and was brought to my senses by Captain M—— whispering my name to a gentleman near him with a ludicrous expression of countenance that amazed me. I instantly remembered the wig, sought for it where it was not to be found; at last got a glimpse of it in my bonnet, clapped it on my head awry, and rushed out till I had got it fairly adjusted." It is in the nature of things that there should be a great many *wig stories;* one we remember which relates a similar accident, but its denouement was more embarrassing to the minister than in the Doctor's case. On entering a church, a certain minister, who prided himself on punctuality, observed, to his horror, that by the clock face in the church steeple he was just half an hour later than the usual hour for service. One of the elders came to his relief, assured him that it yet lacked fifteen minutes of the time, and that what had caused his alarm was but a painted clock. This only added fuel to the flame, and brought down on the Elder's head a sharp rebuke for allowing "a lie" to be imprinted on the front of the church. As he entered the vestry door, some inches too low for his clerical head, hat and wig came to grief on the floor, when the Elder improved the occasion by remarking how much more sinful it was for a minister to carry "a lie" on the top of his head than to have one painted on a church steeple. But no one ever doubted for a moment Dr. Mathieson's "honesty." This was one of his noblest qualities. You know always and exactly where to find him. He was perfectly incapable of playing the hypocrite.

The chief obstacle in the way of twelve months leave of absence to the minister of St. Andrew's Church was the impossibility at that time of finding "supply" for his pulpit. In the summer of 1837, however, the Rev. Robert Neil, now of Seymour, arrived in Canada under the auspices of the Glasgow Colonial Society; with him an arrangement was made to supply the church for six months, and in July Dr. Mathieson took his departure for Scotland, bearing with him a general commission to watch over the interests of the Canadian Synod, and not without an eye to "a little matter of his own," which he wished and hoped to accomplish at the same time. But, though he pressed both his "suits" with exemplary diligence and warmth, it does not appear that in either of them he was very successful. On the contrary, by his own shewing, baffled plans and blighted hopes conspired to throw his mind "into a sad jumble of incongruities." But it was not an unrelieved darkness that set in upon his soul. There was never absent from his mind a deep conviction of the wisdom and goodness of the Creator in *all* his dealings with his creatures. What phrenologists call the bump of veneration was in him largely developed, manifesting itself specially in his love of God, "as God," and then "to the King, as supreme; or unto Governors as unto them that are sent by him."* It has been beautifully said that "the darkest cloud has its silver lining," and of the truth of which he at this time received a very pleasing and convincing illustration. Being present at the University of Glasgow on the day on which the Duke of Montrose was installed as Chancellor, Mr. Mathieson, without previous intimation, had the honour of hearing his name announced among the names of others on whom the degree of Doctor in Divinity had been conferred. "It is well," says a chronicler of the event, "that no permission had been sought for, for it is more than probable Dr. Mathieson's innate modesty of character would have inclined him to shrink from accepting such a well-deserved honour." †

To rid him of the "doldrums" he resolved upon a change of scene and planned a short excursion to the continent. On the 18th April, 1838, he writes from Paris:—"In one of those fits of fancy which sometimes seize me I have been transported to the capital of 'La Belle France.' The steamboat in which I crossed was crowded with cockneys availing themselves of the Easter holidays. Perhaps at some other time I would have mightily enjoyed this assemblage, and the truly ludicrous scenes enacted, but I was too indisposed to relish them. My *debut* was made in the market place of Boulogne, and never was I in such an assemblage of the woman-kind. I am sure there were three or four thousand. A parcel of uglier women I never beheld. What a chattering and

---

* 1 Peter ii. 13.
† Fennings Taylor.

grimace! I was almost convinced of the truth of the argument that no women get to heaven, since there was silence there for half an hour,* for I am sure it would have been impossible to have chained the tongues of the jabbering Boulognese even for that length of time. On my arrival in Paris, as a good ' Doctor' should, my first visit was to the Church, alas! not with the feelings and purposes I ought to have gone thither; but, truly, among the most devout was little devotion seen. The mummery of the Romish Church has a hardening influence on the head and conscience, and some of its grosser absurdities are seen and unsparingly satirized by its own adherents. I was much tickled with two paintings in the gallery of the Louvre: one, a jolly rubicund priest confessing a beautiful young girl—the expression of countenance looking askance through the grated bars of the confessional was admirably hit; in the other, he was confessing an old woman, but here the intense enquiring eye was shut, and the countenance was expressive of utter inanity. The palaces are noble structures. The galleries of Fine Arts are splendid. The churches gorgeous; the music is entrancing; in short, a thousand things excite the astonishment of the stranger and give a peculiarity of character to the city which no one can form an idea of till it is seen." Of course our friend had his *frog story* and it was a good one, but we must cut it short. A Scotchman who was with him at a restaurant had in vain attempted to make himself understood. He wanted " a mutton chop." Had he called for a " beef steak," he would have got it and no mistake, but " mutton chop " was an unsolvable conundrum. High words

---

* Revelations, viii. 1.

followed, which, happily, neither party understood, when at last the despairing Scotchman thundered out, "gin ye canna mak a mutton chope, bring ben onything that 'll fill the kyte o' a hungry man, bit a frôg—you French craters eat frôgs—but a' canna stammac a frôg." This caused such a roar of laughter from the rest of the party as almost frightened the Frenchman out of his propriety. The Doctor set out for Strasbourgh—a distance of over three hundred and fifty miles—travelling by Diligence, railways being then unknown. He had no intention of stopping by the way, but, feeling somewhat fatigued, decided to stay over a day in Nancy, said to be the most beautiful city in France.

He was the rather induced to do this because, otherwise, he must part with some agreeable travelling companions—a Swiss gentleman, and his accomplished and lovely niece, with whom, to tell the truth, the Doctor had fallen desperately in love. In after years he seemed to recal this incident of travel with unspeakable pleasure and many a time, in the honesty of his heart, he recounted it by his fireside with inimitable pathos and vivacity. It may be told now in his own words: "I dare say the *true* reason of my remaining at Nancy was to enjoy the company of a beautiful Swiss girl—a lovelier creature I have seldom looked upon. Such a pair of eyes I have only seen once before that could match them. Her upper lip is the only imperfect feature of her face; it is itself beautiful, but she pouts it out so as to resemble the huge bristling moustache of her uncle, for whom she seems to have a perfect veneration. She is the daughter of a Protestant clergyman; has been staying in France with her uncle, and is now on her way back to her native land. She can neither understand my language, though in the sweetest

tones imaginable she tells me I haef understand a leetle English—
a leetle verry'—nor can I make out what she says, though she
repeats in German and French what she wishes me to know, but
still we found enough of words to become great friends. I know
not whether the coach inclined more to the side I was upon than
that on which her uncle was seated, but when she sunk into sleep—
for we travelled the whole night long—her head always fell softly on
my shoulder—I almost wished the day had never dawned, it bore
so sweet a burden. With sorrow of heart I parted with her, and I
think nothing but the small stock of money in my purse prevented
me from accompanying her to Switzerland. Indeed I felt that I
could have travelled the world over with her." The expression
" *leetle verry* " occurs in many of his letters, and with some of his
friends it was a standing joke which he always heartily enjoyed.

The Doctor was not much enamoured with French scenery, and
still less so with the natives—"a chattering unprincipled set of creatures whose politeness is grimace." One trait of genuine feeling,
however, he observed in the Cemetery of Père La Chasse. "I was
admiring the beautiful simplicity of an inscription on a tomb-stone
of unaffected neatness—'*A Mon Amie*'—when a youth came with
a garland, placed it on the grave, shed a few tears—I thought they
were sincere—plucked a flower—heart's-ease—and departed."

He arrived at Strasbourgh on the 2nd of May. It was the
Fête of Louis Philip. "After breakfast I visited the Cathedral,
one of the most beautiful specimens of Gothic architecture in
France. Upwards of four thousand troops attended Mass. They
occupied in one dense column the nave. Nothing was seen but
the glittering bayonets. The soft low notes of the great organ

alternating with its swelling thunders pealing along the vaulted roofs—now and then interrupted by the full blasts of the horns and the rattling drums of a large military band, had a novel and grand effect, but very inappropriate to that Being who must be worshipped in spirit and in truth. After service the troops were reviewed in the great square of the city. Next came an aquatic spectacle, when gay galleys floated on the river. In the evening the city was brilliantly illuminated. I speak within bounds when I say that thousands of rockets were in the air at the same moment. The blaze of light vied with meridian sunbeams. The exhibitions of Vauxhall are not for a moment to be compared with this in respect of grandeur and effect. Torches glared amid the trees, under the soft foliage of which thousands of all classes roamed, and, among them, the " *leetle verry*," her uncle, and I. Next morning they went off to Basle, not without warmly inviting me to accompany them. I saw those Swiss mountains in the distance amid which my imagination had oftentimes pictured many a lovely scene. I was sorely tempted to go, and my *cara amica* urged her request by representing the pleasure it would give to her aged father to meet with a Protestant clergyman from another country. But it was fated that we should part. It was the only really pleasing incident met with since I came to France—brief and beautiful it has passed away like one of those sunbeams that flit o'er the fields in Autumn—but, like the fields it has contributed to ripen, the remembrance of it may give a melancholy delight to the coming winter of a life which threatens to be gloomy."

It was now within a short time of the meeting of the General

Assembly in Edinburgh, and our traveller must retrace his steps. On his homeward way he arrived by Diligence in an old town in Normandy about five o'clock one morning. The driver endeavoured to inform him when he would start again; the hour he understood to be half-past seven. Desirous of seeing as much of the quaint old town as possible, he "did" the cathedral and some other ancient edifices and returned to the hotel at seven, but to his unutterable mortification learned that the Diligence had left nearly half-an-hour before, carrying off his valise in which was *all* his money, some thirty sovereigns! What to do he knew not. In a strange land, unable to speak the language of its people, and without a penny in his pocket, what *could* he do? "Without a morsel to eat," he used to say, "I set out to walk to the next town, some thirty miles off, with feelings that I cannot express, fearing that I might have to foot it to Calais, and even beyond, and beg my bread as I went along. By the way I suffered much from the great heat and dust, from thirst and hunger. Though soon foot-sore and weary I pushed along, and by night-fall arrived at the inn where I was told the Diligence would stop. I quickly entered, and in the corner of a common room among a heap of baggage espied my valise, which I instantly took possession of and transferred the 'treasure trove' to my depleted pockets."

The General Assembly of the Church of Scotland met then, as it does still, on the third Thursday of May. Under any circumstances the Doctor would have strained a point to be in "Auld Reekie" on that august occasion, but a variety of personal considerations conspired to render his attendance at this time particularly desirable if not absolutely necessary. He had taken

K

a rather inconsiderate step by resigning his charge in Montreal, and must now seek the aid of his friends and patrons in his endeavours to secure another "living." The ordeal through which he must needs pass was to be severe and humbling, yet it proved a salutary one, and in the end, was greatly conducive to his future happiness. For some months about this time he acknowledges that he was "the most miserable man upon earth," and certainly for a time he allowed his feelings to get the better of his judgment, and gave reins to the gloomy forebodings of a sensitive mind by entertaining proposals which sober reflection convinced him were "visionary and absurd." We have already hinted the existence of a tender attachment for "somebody" in whom were bound up his brightest hopes of domestic bliss and happiness. It is time now to speak more plainly and admit the existence of a long-continued, pure, and ardent affection for one whom he fondly hoped to become one day his "*alter ego.*" But those hopes were now dissipated and blasted, and he had to drain the bitter cup of disappointment to the dregs as best he could. We need not be more particular, but this explanation seems necessary in order to account for the then unsettled state of his mind and purposes, which otherwise were unintelligible. We can now the better understand the following extract from a letter dated the 2nd July, 1838:—"You will have heard that I have resigned my situation in Montreal. This you will, no doubt, censure as a foolish and indiscreet act, but circumstanced as I am, and feeling as I do, it appears differently to myself. Even as it respects my congregation it appears to me justifiable. In returning to them unmarried I feel that I neither could be happy nor so useful to them as otherwise I might be. But, as I could not offer such an excuse, I eagerly embraced a momentary feeling of dissatisfaction which they expressed for my being so long absent as a reason for doing that which on other grounds I had contemplated to do." The Doctor was right in supposing that his long absence was the cause of the disaffection in his congregation, and that it was only momentary, for he never lost the affections of his people nor did his own heart ever grow cold to them—a life-long and romantic attachment subsisted between the minister and people of St. Andrew's congregation—nor does it appear that the resignation referred to was accepted or even seriously entertained by them. But the Doctor had acted in good faith, was ready to accept the consequences, and immediately "went into the business of canvassing for a kirk." But he had calculated without his host. Never was there a man worse fitted for the business. He had influential friends in the Duke of Arygle, Lord Strathmore, the Oswalds, Fox Maule, Dr. John Lee, Principal McFarlan and others, but, unfortunately for the Doctor's prospects, these were all on *the wrong side of politics*. Besides, his own proud and independent spirit stood in the way of preferment. Though he was on the leet of some of the best parishes in Scotland he would not stoop to preach, as a candidate, a *trial sermon*. Not he. Bravo, Doctor! After two months of keen application, during which he suffered "unspeakable misery," he desisted from further attempts in that direction, and contented himself with making this note of his failure :—" Perhaps Principal Macfarlan had as much influence in the way of Church preferments as any other, but he failed in my case. Perhaps he had not a proper presentable man—but in my own opinion, in these days, I could have stood alongside of any of my neighbours, though this may be a little of the air of Canada that I have caught. It was, I believe, the most anxious wish of the old Principal's heart to get me home, and on his death-bed he regretted that he had not been able to accomplish this." He was now fairly launched on the tempestuous ocean of life, and abandoned himself to the mercy of the billows. He had been taught to regard great men's promises as the most unsubstantial of all unsubstantial things, and disinterested patronage as one of the rarest things in human intercourse. Oppressed with the intended good offices of his friends he was disposed to prefer the petition of another who in similar circumstances prayed, "God defend me from my friends, I can defend myself from my enemies." The General Assembly had decided to extend their Indian Mission to Ceylon. As the drowning man clutches a straw, so the Doctor, in his anxiety to leave the scene of his disappointments and to escape the interrogations which a return to Montreal would give rise to, made application, and was appointed as missionary to that distant field. But he had yet to be taught in the school of adversity. "I think I mentioned," he writes to a friend, "that I had been recently appointed to the East Indies, and would probably take my departure immediately, but my confounded pride is at work again, and obstacles are raised up which have already marred my intentions. I found, that though I had been nominated to the station, I must receive my *appointment* through the Presbytery of Quebec. This proposal I spurned, declaring my willingness to go on my own responsibility, but I was made to know that I could not go in this way without running the risk of being excised from the Church altogether. As I have no desire to bid the 'Auld Lady' (Mother Church) so unceremoniously good-by, I am now turning my attention to another quarter of the world—Demerara and the Mauritius—and have come to the resolution of preparing myself for the latter, on the contingency of my appointment being certain. If my proposal is acceded to I will proceed immediately to Paris and study the French language, or, perhaps go and see " *leetle verry* "; she will be a delightful instructor."

While these conflicting plans and purposes were perplexing the Doctor's mind he received an "unexpected deluge" of letters from Montreal from many of his people, expressing the continued affection of the whole congregation towards him and urging his return. This was in September. On the 8th of October he was aboard the good ship "Oxford" bound for Canada, and in due time, to use his own quotation, " Richard's himself again ! "

On the 30th of July, 1840, Dr. Mathieson was married, by the Rev. Henry Esson, to Catherine Elizabeth, daughter of Mr. John Mackenzie, of Montreal. It was a happy union, for, in the partner of his maturer years were sweetly blended those christian graces and accomplishments which his youthful imagination had many years before pictured to itself as indispensible to his ide of holy matrimony.

> " At length his heart
> Upon a fellow mortal's answering breast
> Could shed its tears of joy "

in a sense that he had never known till now he had "a home" in Canada; a blythe and peaceful home it was, as all can testify who were privileged to enter it, and its portals were as cheerfully opened to the poorest in the parish as to the representatives of wealth and high degree. He had a family of two sons and four daughters. On the 21st of March, 1847, death invaded his dwelling and took from him his dear little daughter Nancy Fisher, aged three years and three months. The good Doctor's love for children was remarkable in one who had been so long a "Benedict." He coveted no better society than theirs. In their company and listening to their innocent prattle he could sit for hours, and he himself became young again. To play dominoes with them, or tell them mirth-provoking stories, to sing for them, or dressing up his thumbs with handkerchiefs, to amuse them with pantomimic illustrations of "Punch and Judy," was his delight; nor was it forgotten to dismiss them with a kind word—a little seed-thought—suitable to the occasion and the capacity of his little audience. Proportionate to the love he bore them were the tenderest emotions of his heart touched when his Heavenly Father saw fit to create the first blank in his own family circle. "On a Saturday night at 10 o'clock the physician called and left no room for hope. She was sinking rapidly. With a heavy heart next morning I went to church, afraid of allowing personal feelings to intermingle with the duties of God's house. I prayed for sustaining grace and preached an old but an appropriate sermon—'Not my will but thine be done.' The sermon was solemn and the congregation attentive. I hardly expected to find my sweet loved Nancy in the land of the living on my return. She was much worse, but still perfectly sensible. I lay down on the bed beside her, and, trying to hide my tears, spoke to her of God, and heaven, and of the love of Jesus. She became weaker as the night wore on, and ere the day dawned my beloved child drew her last breath. Mortal life was gone, the endless life in Jesus Christ begun. The body of corruption, still dear to us, shall be raised up a glorified body, incorruptible by the mighty power by which Christ subdues all things to himself. Precious are the consolations of the gospel in such an hour as this. May the Holy Spirit descend upon us and effectually apply them!"

Under date the 1st of January, 1848, occurs this further allusion to his bereavement and evidence of his desire to profit by it: "God has been pleased to spare me to see the beginning of another year. Often during the course of the last have I thought that this was what I could not expect. O that I were sufficiently thankful, and that He would enable me to be more faithful in His service than in times past, if it be His will to spare me to my family and for the accomplishment of whatsoever He may be pleased to honour me as an instrument of carrying out. My family, and friends are in the enjoyment of good health and happiness. Our beloved child has been taken from us—she is not forgotten, but remembered with deep sorrow. The whole of life is but a dream. O that God would enable us to realize this, and prepare for joining those whom in His love He has removed from us. Many, innumerable blessings have I to be thankful for—my kind, affectionate flock, their indulgence and benevolence not the least."

CHAPTER VI.

PARISH WORK. REVISITS SCOTLAND. DEATH OF MRS. MATHIESON. LIFE AT BEECHRIDGE. DEATH OF JANET EWING MATHIESON.

It was in 1849, while comparatively a young man yet, at the age of forty-six, that Dr. Mathieson had the first premonitions of disease in his own frame. He began to feel unequal to the unaided work of the pastoral superintendence of so large a congregation as St. Andrew's had become. There were now nearly five hundred on the roll of communicants. His people were widely scattered, many of them living far outside the city limits, which rendered his visits to them irksome and tedious. The labour, too, of preparing his discourses became more onerous, for while he never neglected his habit of careful preparation, nor ever appeared in the pulpit without a clean copy of his sermon *in extenso*—and his caligraphy was beautiful—his ideas began to flow less rapidly, and there was less of the *currente calamo* in the hand that once could dash off a discourse at a sitting; and its delivery came to be followed by a depression, and sometimes a faintness that distressed him. Here is the brief record of a week's work at this time: "Monday till Friday, not much done, though always busy; a number of sick visits; several funerals; very little fatigues me now. Saturday—study; wrought hard and constant till one in the morning; sermon not finished. Sabbath—at work in the morning; discourse *long enough* but not finished; must make a practical application on the value of the soul, the great motive of missionary and ministerial labour. In better spirits to-day; very warm; my voice failed me; violent palpitation at the heart and quick breathing from the slightest exertion. My work, I fear, is drawing to a close. The summer ended! Alas, how little done! I begin to feel a deeper responsibility, but, if I can judge my heart, my desire is to present my dear people to Christ. Lord, increase my faith, make me more earnest, let me offend none, conciliate all. It pains me much that some have left the church whose countenance and friendship would have been encouraging; but thanks be to God that a numerous and attached people remains under my ministry, bless it, O bless it unto them! The feeblest instrumentality is strong when Thou, O Lord, art with us. Stir up Thy might, and save and bless."

Dr. Mathieson was too honest a man to appropriate to himself, or try to pawn off upon his hearers, the thoughts of another without due acknowledgment. With one single exception, which in after years he used to recount with inimitable humour, and, when told in the hearing of a brother cleric, always coupled with the admonition "be sure your sin will find you out," he was blameless of the charge of plagiarism. He admitted that upon a certain occasion, from sheer want of time to prepare a discourse, he had "taken in" a pretty large portion of a sermon that he had heard preached in Scotland ere he came to Canada, and which, unfortunately for him, had found its way, in print, into the hands of a lady belonging to his congregation with whom he was on intimate terms of friendship. She only, of all that heard the Doctor preach that day, detected the theft, but she was too true a friend to make mention of it to others. She was too polite, moreover, to make direct allusion to it in after conversation with her minister, but, from a casual remark or two that escaped her, the Doctor was convinced in his own mind that she was perfectly cognizant of his "crime," and he there and then resolved that it was the last time he should ever be found in a similar predicament.

Little do most of us know of the arduous process undergone in that laboratory of thought, the parson's study, in the "getting up' of two discourses such as a man of scholarly attainments would wish to utter in the hearing of an intelligent, educated, and, perhaps, a critical congregation. It is so usual to speak of a sermon as a thing that a minister can shake out of his coat sleeve at any time, on the shortest notice, that one requires to get a peep behind the scenes to realize the amount of hard work involved. One of our best sermon writers, who has had upwards of thirty years' experience, assures us that it costs him "as many hours of hard labour to make a sermon, worth the name, as it costs any carpenter to make a door, or any cabinet-maker a chair. And, if I sit down to the more pretentious work of writing a book, who will say that I am not undertaking labour which would cost me as many days of toil, and occasion me as much fatigue, in the long run, as would be incurred by the ten or dozen mechanics who should undertake the construction of a steam engine, always supposing my book would be worth reading."*

* Dr. Jenkins on "the dignity of labour," in *Presbyterian*, January, 1869.

PARISH WORK AND DOMESTIC AFFLICTION.

A celebrated painter, on being asked how he mixed his colours to secure such marvellous effect, is said to have replied, "I mix them, sir, with my brains." We need not pursue the analogy further than to remark that a sermon without brains is a very meagre affair, not in the least degree likely to reach the hearts of those who listen to it. Dr. Mathieson's sermons were not of this discription. Viewed as mere literary compositions they were elaborate essays; carefully thought out and beautifully expressed. Some of them, indeed, were so in an exceptional degree. We might instance three discourses, preached in the ordinary course of his ministry, and which were afterwards printed in "the fall of the leaf," which fully bear us out in what we say of his composition, and yet there are others which, perhaps, in this regard, were even more worthy of preservation. While no one could be more deeply impressed with the duty of careful preparation, we cannot but admire the playful allusion to his efforts in that direction:—

"Knowing that I must be absent for three days of the week previous to communion, I set down to my preparations the preceding week, but *necessity* not applying vigorously her lash, procrastination whispered enticingly, ' there is time enough yet :' so very little was done. I started for ——, made —— and his spouse happy, got a jolly fee, the largest I ever got, and returned to Montreal on Wednesday with a fearful cold in my head. But the next day, when I had resolved to begin work in right earnest, was wholly taken up with other duties. Poor —— had died, and was to be buried on that day. His mother was in dreadful affliction, and his father utterly cast down, so I resolved to visit them before the funeral. The day was very wet, and going to the cemetery I got more cold, with considerable fever. On Friday I had to *set to*, besides the work for Sunday, having to select and *dress a calf* for this evening's repast, as A. K. H. B.* would designate the immature production of an earlier day, and having the same *veal* as an offering to present to my people on the following days. In desperation I telegraphed to Quebec and had a favourable reply from Dr. Cook, and so set to work with all fury and had my sermon finished by midnight. The Doctor arrived early on Sabbath morning, and I laid on him, table service, concluding address, evening service, and Monday's. From the excitement I felt well, but with sad revulsion on Tuesday, and I have scarcely been out of the house since."

This may be the proper place to refer to Dr. Mathieson's printed sermons. They are twelve in number, and were delivered in the following order :

1. 1827, April 8th. On the occasion of Mr. Wat-on's death, from JEREMIAH IX. 21 : " For death hath come up into our windows."

2. 1836, November 30th. Preached before the St. Andrew s Society, Montreal, from PSALM CXXXVII. 1-6 : " By the rivers of Babylon, there we sat down, yea, we wept, when we remembered Zion " &c.

3. 1843, October 22nd. Delivered on board the transport ship "Java," off Quebec, to the 1st Battalion 71st Highland Light Infantry, *en route* to the West Indies, from 2nd COR. XIII.

---

* The reference here is to a curious article " concerning veal " in " The Recreations of a Country Parson," by the Rev. Andrew K. H. Boyd, then minister of St. Bernard, Edinburgh, and now of St. Andrews.

2: " Finally, brethren, farewell, " &c.: also, ACTS XX. 32: " And now, brethren, I commend you to God and the word of his grace," &c.

4. 1848, May 21st. The Christian's death no cause for sorrow. On the occasion of Miss Spier's death, from JEREMIAH XXII. 10: " Weep ye not for the dead," &c., also Revelations XIV. 13: " Blessed are the dead who die in the Lord," &c.

5. ⎧ 1849. The moral and religious influences of autumn. A
6. ⎨ sermon in three parts, preached on three several Sabbaths "in
7. ⎩ the fall of the leaf," from ISAIAH LXIV. 6: " We all do fade as a leaf."

8. 1852. A tribute of respect to the memory of a good man; preached on the occasion of the death of Mr. Hugh Brodie, the " faithful Elder " who accompanied Dr. Mathieson in many of his missionary excursions to the valley of the Chateauguay. ACTS XI. 24: " For he was a good man."

9. 1861. Preached, 29th May, in St. Andrew's Church, Quebec, at the opening of the Synod, from ACTS IV. 19, 20: " Whether it be right in the sight of God to hearken unto you more than unto God, judge ye: for we cannot but speak the things which we have seen and heard."

10. 1863. Preached, 30th November, before the St. Andrew's Society, from PSALM. XLVII. 12 13: " Walk about Zion, and go round about her, tell the towers thereof," &c.

11. 1864. The vanity of earthly objects of attachment; preached on the occasion of the death of Mr. James Hervey, and printed for private distribution, from PSALM LXXXVIII. 18: " Lover

and friend hast thou put far from me, and mine acquaintance into darkness."

12. 1868. Preached on St. Andrew's Day, in the St. Andrew's Church, before the St. Andrew's Society of Montreal, from PSALM XLVII. 12, 13, 14 : " Walk about Zion," &c.

In addition to his written sermons, Dr. Mathieson has left behind him an amount of manuscript large enough to fill many volumes, exhibiting an ease and grace of diction, a knowledge of men and things in general, an acquaintance with literature, and a grasp of mind and thought, that would have gained him eminence as a man of letters had he aspired to authorship. His writings are chiefly in the form of letters, some of an official character, others of a private nature; many of them are at once interesting and amusing, from the graphic manner in which contemporaneous events are noticed, not a few of them contain information of value to the future historian of the Church. In his youthful days he was addicted to poetry, and he could also wield the pencil of the caricaturist with considerable effect; but to these accomplishments his own graver thoughts attached small importance. " The verses you thought so pretty," he says, " were destroyed many years ago when I thought I was going to ' the Land o' the Leal.' I do not know that you will be able to find a single couplet from my pen anywhere except some extemporaneous effusions occasionally in letters to my friends. I wrote for my own amusement. There were many little pieces that I have often deeply regretted having destroyed, but I had no ambition they should survive me. I was proud of the fire-side praise, but desired no more, and committed my papers wholesale to the flames, being too weak to undergo the fatigue of making a selection, and would not for the world have any knave laugh at my follies after I had taken wing."

From what has been said it may be inferred that the matter of Dr. Mathieson's sermons was generally good and oft times rose to brilliancy and genuine eloquence. His manner of delivery was pleasing, though at times marred by a hesitancy of utterance, chiefly caused by a peculiarity of vision—a near-sightedness, which defied the skill of the most scientific optician to remedy, and which prevented him from deciphering his own legible manuscript, without which, except on baptismal and communion occasions, he never attempted to speak from the pulpit. He had early prepared his congregation for the reception of " read discourses " and defended himself against the possible assailants of " paper ministers," as may be seen on reference to the first sermon which he preached in Montreal, and which is hereto appended, where allusion is made to his constitutional inability to " mandate " his discourses. " The time taken in mandating a discourse I would consider more profitably employed, both for myself and the people I instruct, in acquiring a more extensive knowledge of Scripture truths, and in composing clear, well connected, and interesting discourses." This deficiency, for such he acknowledged it to be, was less regretted by himself than by his friends, and was a subject on which he allowed himself to be twitted very often without in the least discomposing him. Upon occasions when conversation took that direction, and he thought it advisable to change the subject, he usually brought down the company with a hearty laugh over the story of two old wives in Scotland who had a holy horror of "readers." They had gone together to hear a sermon preached by a blind minister, and both agreed that it was "a gran' discoorse." The fact of the preacher's blindness, however, had remained undiscovered to the one, who, on their homeward way asked her companion did she think "that yon sermon was read?" "Na, na, replied the other, that couldna be, for *the man's blinn.*" "Blinn said ye," retorted her interrogator, "*than a wuss they were a' blinn.*"

The brief extract from his journal which now follows may suffice to indicate the kind of work to which the city minister is sometimes called, and the scenes he sometimes witnesses. (1849) "Sent for to visit a sick person—horrid scene! Ushered into a garret, on the bare floor of which, covered with rags, lay a dying creature who had had a religious education but seemed to have lived long in neglect of God, as I learned from others, for she was insensible and within two hours of being called to judgment. Her husband was a ragged, squallid wretch, on whom want and drunkenness had entailed disease. Around her there were half a dozen women, dirty and ragged, and reeling with drink. A rough block of wood covered with a rag was her pillow. It was heart-sickening. I prayed with the poor creature—utterly insensible I fear to any religious consolation—addressed those around in terms of christian pity and warning, mingled with reproach, but seemingly to no purpose. There is room for reflection here—room for censure somewhere. Why such brutish conduct, such induration of heart, such drunkenness, filth, forgetfulness of God? Why should these be left to pursue such courses without determined efforts to reclaim them? What is to be done? Already staggering under the load of duty and anxiety I feel that I must break down, unless I find relief. Yet, work I must. The Lord make me faithful. Let me not shrink, however toilsome the labour, or disgusting the scenes. Strengthen me with Thy strength; guide me with Thy wisdom; pour into my soul a portion of the Saviour's zeal for perishing souls. We have the engine that will yet move the world, let us apply it......A rich, friendless, man may find flatterers, a poor man, no sympathy from his associates. This man could find no one to aid him in carrying his wife to the grave—human sympathy is gone because he is in rags. He *is* a useless wretch to be sure, but surely not so bad as to deprive him of pity in affliction. Gave him five shillings to buy a coffin and one shilling and three-pence for a cart hire—" The richman died: *and was buried!*"

To obtain a temporary respite from work, and in the hope of re-establishing his health, the Doctor bethought him once more of the only remedy in which he had much faith, and the very anticipation of which was as " the balm of Gilead" to his downcast soul— a trip to Scotland. Having made the necessary arrangements for the supply of his pulpit, he accordingly " went home " in the year 1852, and, after spending a pleasant summer, during which he visited the three Kingdoms, and had the honour of addressing the General Assembly, he returned to Canada with greatly invigorated health. It was during this visit that he secured the services of his first assistant, the Rev. Robert Dobie, then assistant to Principal Haldane of St. Andrew's, and now the minister of Lindsay, Ontario. This arrangement proved satisfactory while it lasted, but was of short duration, for Mr. Dobie, having received a call to Osnabruck, resigned connection with St. Andrew's congregation, and for six long years Dr. Mathieson strove manfully to accom plish, alone, that which experience had convinced him was work enough for two ministers.

In the meantime our friend was subjected to the saddest and most severe trial which it was possible for him to suffer. As " friend after friend departs," the minister of a large congregation must needs revisit oft the city of the dead. The way to the cemetery—that sleeping place,

" where servants, masters, small and great,
partake the same repose—"

becomes a familiar road, lined as it were with the memories of those who have been borne to the tomb. Along this road Dr. Mathieson had now to follow the remains of his dear wife to the silent grave. She died on the 29th of February, 1856, aged thirty-three after a long illness, borne with Christian fortitude and resignation to the divine will. The brief epitaph inscribed on a monumental tablet that was erected by her friends on the wall of St. Andrew's Church, near the pulpit, records that she was " endeared to all who knew her by a kind disposition and the lively interest which he manifested in the prosperity of this Church." She was a most devoted, affectionate wife, and the very embodiment of maternal love — gentle, guileless, and sincerely pious, but who never made any parade of religious feeling. In a letter written to a friend in Scotland shortly after her death, the Doctor thus alludes to his bereavement—" you will deeply sympathize with me when I inform you that she who was nearest and dearest to me has been removed from the troubles of this life to the enjoyment—we have no doubt—of a better. Her last end was peaceful and calm, indeed I have seldom witnessed a more sublime spectacle of faith and hope and resignation. Her confidence in her Saviour's love, and longing to be with Him, has infused great consolation into the cup of sorrow given us to drink. There was a heroism in her whole conduct and an undoubting trust in her Redeemer that seemed to me to be a special vouchsafement from our Heavenly Father—as a testimony to herself, and to us, that she was accepted by Him through Christ. Her unceasing prayer during the last night of her illness was, " come, Lord Jesus, come quickly !" I cannot yet realize the terrible desolation in our affections occasioned by the absence of her who was the spirit and life of all our household joys. God's will be done."

The Rev. Robert Herbert Story, the son of his old valued friend, became Dr. Mathieson's assistant in May, 1859; but on the death of his father, having received a presentation to the parish of Roseneath, his engagement with St. Andrew's Church necessarily terminated. In the following spring, the Rev. James Kerr arrived as assistant, and remained about a year, when he returned to Scotland. Some years afterwards he and his young wife took passage on board the steamship "London," which foundered in the Bay of Biscay, on her voyage to Australia, and they shared the melancholy fate of many others, who sank into a watery grave.

The Rev. W. M. Inglis, now minister of St. Andrew's Church, Kingston, was Dr. Mathieson's next assistant and remained in Montreal, till August, 1863. The Rev. Andrew Paton succeeded him in November, 1864, and, after the lapse of a year, was requested to accept a permanent appointment as "assistant and successor." Having received ordination thereto from the Presbytery of Kinross, he was inducted on the 14th of February,

1866. The circumstances connected with his demission of the charge are so exceptional, and withal so honourable to Mr. Paton, as justify us in giving them a place here in connection with the history of the congregation.

Mr. Paton had been on a visit to Scotland during the summer (1869); was present at the General Assembly, where he delivered an address in relation to the position of the Canadian Church, and had returned to his duties in the month of October. On the 18th of November, he had given notice to the Presbytery of Montreal, of his intention to ask leave to be released from his present charge, although he had then no immediate prospect of obtaining another. On the evening of the very same day he received a telegraph message by the Atlantic Cable, offering him a presentation to the parish of Penpont, in Dumfriesshire. On the 23rd, the day before the burning of the Church, he received another message intimating that he had been appointed to the charge. It is important that Dr. Mathieson's estimate of his last assistant should be preserved, and here are his first impressions of him as communicated to a friend, under date the 13th October, 1864: "My assistant arrived last week and preached an excellent plain discourse last Sabbath. I was highly pleased with him. I was not well enough to go out in the evening, but am told his discourse was superior to that of the morning. He is a gentlemanly, unpretending man, frank, and anxious to approve himself in all departments of duty as a good workman. I think I shall get along with him very agreeably." At a meeting of the congregation, held prior to Mr. Paton's departure, Dr. Mathieson alluded very feelingly to the relations which had existed between himself and Mr. Paton; and

PARISH WORK AND DOMESTIC AFFLICTION.

to the efficient manner in which he had always fulfilled his duties. Nor were substantial proofs awanting that his services had been appreciated by the congregation, and that their best wishes followed him to his new sphere of labour.

During the last ten years of his life Dr. Mathieson was in the habit of spending the greater portion of the summer months upon his farm, at Beechridge, about five and twenty miles distant from the city. There was nothing about the place, or its vicinity, that one could have supposed would have had any attractions for a mind so poetic and so keenly appreciative of the beautiful in nature. To our own eye, though we saw it in winter, the locality seemed a dull and dreary solitude, fitted rather as a place of endurable exile than for a pleasant summer retreat. It was inland and the landscape, unrelieved by hill or dale, was fringed by the grim, gray primeval forest. But here the old Doctor had a snug little cottage, and a hundred acres of land that he could call his own. He had his garden in which to delve, and the woods through which he could saunter and meditate without fear of being disturbed by the ceaseless din of the busy town or the ringing of the door bell. He was not far from the manse, where he could always reckon on a hearty welcome, and he took great pleasure in the society and companionship of its kind and hospitable inmates. He loved the country, "for God made the country, man made the town." If any one spoke disparagingly of it in his presence he would join with his old friend Virgil, and exclaim, " *O fortunatos nimium, sua si bona norint, agricolas.*" * Happy as the Mantuan

---

* "O thrice happy farmers, did they but know their own blessings."

bard, under shade of his own "beech tree," he enjoyed "rustic ease," as thoroughly as ever Horace did when on his Sabine farm he quaffed his "mild falernian." There was little to give variety to his thoughts, saving the sound of the postman's horn that daily woke up to the echoes of the woods. Then there was a rush for the post-office in expectation of letters from Montreal, or from Scotland, or, perhaps, the much-coveted, and long-looked for epistle from his dear friend Gregory Wortabet, "the Syrian exile." Much of his time must have been spent in writing, for he had a host of correspondents, and it is worthy of remark, as illustrative of his exact and methodical habits, that of every letter he wrote, he kept a verbatim copy, and that almost every letter received by him was preserved, labelled, and so carefully fyled that at any time he could refer to it.

Only one incident has come to our knowledge in connection with his quiet life at Beechridge, that appeared helpful "to adorn a tale," and we are not quite sure that the Doctor would have liked to have seen it in print. But as it tends to display two very characteristic traits of his character, we feel justified in making allusion to it. Personal courage and benevolence were stamped on Dr. Mathieson's countenance. So erect was his carriage, so martial his bearing, so measured his step, that, but for his clerical habit, it might be said of him that he was "every inch a soldier." His bravery was not of that kind that tempted him to rush recklessly into danger, but, rather, a ready resource and presence of mind in the hour of danger that never failed him. In no circumstances was he known to betray unmanly alarm. During the time of the rebellion he declared himself willing to doff his cassock, shoulder a musket, and fight the enemies of his Queen and country. Though, had the necessity for his so doing arisen, it would have pained him grievously, for he had a very high regard for his French Canadian fellow country-men, of whom he said at the time, "Never have there been creatures more belied than they have been. Their nature is peaceable and polite, and, at heart, they are strongly attached to the British Government. They have been sadly duped and misled by designing knaves." But, to our story, a few years ago it was, that the Doctor took his accustomed morning walk into the garden, at Beechridge, where his old servant-man of all work, was busily employed. He thought to have "a crack" with him, but there was something in his gesture and incoherent speech that morning that aroused the Doctor's suspicions. The man had a "wakeness," he knew, rather by report than from personal observation for the old man's respect for "his Reverence" was great and had hitherto sufficed to keep him "within bounds" in the minister's presence. But on this occasion, he had forgotten himself; yet, as the Doctor thought, he was not so "far gone" as to be insensible to a mild rebuke, which was with due solemnity and emphasis administered. Dean Ramsay relates an instance, in which a similar remonstrance had been addressed to a highlander in respect of his partiality for the "mountain dew," in which Donald naively acquiesced under certain reservations, thus : "depend upon it," said Mr. M., "its a bad thing whiskey." "Weel, weel, Sir," replied Donald, "I'll no say but it *may ;*" adding in a very decided tone, "speciallic *baad* whusky." But, our old man was not prepared for even such a qualified admission as that. He became furious, and made a desperate lunge at the

Doctor's person with the pitchfork, which he held in his hands. The Doctor's situation was dangerous in the extreme. No quarter was to be expected from such a foe, even had he felt disposed to shew the white feather. With his stout walking stick, however, he adroitly parried the thrust, and, with the proficiency of an expert, plied his assailant with so rapid a succession of lusty thuds as soon placed him *hors du combat.*

It was a serious matter. The old man was hailed before the magistrate and sent to prison. But the Doctor's goodness of heart was shewn, first, by forwarding the sum of five dollars to provide for the culprit's comfort, and, afterwards, by visiting him in the prison and manifesting a personal interest for his welfare, both in body and soul. It may be added that when his term of imprisonment expired, he resumed his old situation, and, when he heard of his master's death, he wept bitterly, wishing that he himself had gone first, as there would be no one now to care for him.

Before closing what we have called our domestic annals of Dr. Mathieson, we wish to give an extract from a letter of his to a friend, dated the 15th September, 1863. It is worthy of preservation both because of its raciness and humour, and it affords a capitable illustration of the manner in which the Doctor *could* mount his " high horse " when a fitting occasion presented itself. The reference will be quite familiar to the members of his congregation, and we feel sure that not one of them would have us suppress it. It is so characteristic, and so good naturedly told as completely to take the sting out of allusions that might otherwise be regarded as offensive.

" It is now three or four years since I was walking down

Bleury-street, as I fancied, with all the briskness and agility of youth, when I met two old women and heard the one say to the other, "There goes old Dr. Mathieson." Old! said I. Old! The sound was new in my ears, and truly I was not a little mortified in being ranked among the Patriarchs of the age, especially as my friend Muir alleged that I was in hot haste in search of a second wife. Now, to have the prefix *old* to my cognomen would assuredly obscure every chance of success. I naturally thought the old dames delighted in scandal, and to call me old was just a bit of spite on their part. I have had, however, many material proofs since of the truth of their observation. But what is worst of all some worthy members of my Church have discovered that I am getting old, and that "it will be for the benefit of the congregation that I retire," and, in compassion for my infirmities, have thought it *expedient* to offer me £400 per annum for life to induce me quietly to do so. A very nice thing, you will say, and reproachfully ask why I did not at once jump at the offer? Well, my dear friend, I have something of the feeling of youth—if not the activity—about me still, and I would not be so unceremoniously shelved even though they should try to frighten me by telling me that half of the congregation was about to rise in rebellion against the administration of the old fogies, and that it would be better for me to *pocket the affront.* So *I mounted my high horse* and told them I would neither resign the office of minister of St. Andrew's Church, nor *any part* of the authority attached to it, until legally and constitutionally set aside by the Presbytery, that I would neither accept of their bribe nor minister to a dissatisfied people, and not doing the duty, would accept none of the pay, so they might when they pleased look about for another who would please them better, and my connection with them in relation to all active duties would cease on the 24th September. Subsequently, at a meeting of the Elders and Trustees, they repudiated the charge of dissatisfaction to the extent alleged. My first intention was to leave Canada, take a cottage on the banks of the Gairloch, and spend the remainder of my days among some dear friends in peace. When it became known that I was about to leave the country a meeting of the congregation was held and certain resolutions passed, it is said unanimously, highly favourable, nay, very flattering to me. I have not yet seen them, but the probability is I shall remain in Canada for the winter, if not for the rest of my days, which now cannot be very long."

It was at Beechridge that the sad tidings reached Dr. Mathieson of the death, by drowning, of his eldest daughter, Janet Ewing. This distressing occurrence took place on the 29th of July, 1868. In his enfeebled state of health it was a crushing blow to him. Since her mother's death, "Tudy" had been the light of his dwelling, and she was now woman grown, in her twenty-second year. A lovely, amiable, happy creature. She had left him but a few days before, in the full bloom of health, on a short visit to some friends at Cacouna. At high tide she went down to the shore in company with another young lady for the purpose of bathing, and a projecting rock was selected from which they might leap into the water. Miss Mathieson was unusually cheerful and sportive, and was the first to plunge, exultantly, into the wave. She leaped into Eternity! for she sank to rise no more. When assistance arrived it was too late. Life was extinct. The feelings of her aged father may be imagined, but no language could express them, and we search in vain for any written record of emotions that were too deep for utterance.

CHAPTER SEVENTH.

REMINISCENCES.　MR. BETHUNE.　BISHOP STRACHAN.　MESSRS. SPARK, HARKNESS, CONNELL.　ST. ANDREW'S CHURCH.

It was in the beginning of the year 1848 that the *Presbyterian*, a monthly magazine published by the lay Association of Montreal in the interests of the church, was first begun. Dr. Mathieson was during its earlier years a frequent contributor to its columns. In the first number of it there is a long letter, signed N. M. I. L. (*nemo me impune lacessit*) evidently penned by the subject of our biography, in which are detailed a number of useful and interesting fragments of history. To this the Doctor himself referred us for the information that he was possessed of regarding the Rev. John Bethune, who was instrumental in organizing the first Presbyterian Congregation in Montreal, that of St. Gabriel's, in the year 1786. The Church of St. Gabriel, however, was not erected until 1792. It was the first Presbyterian Church erected in British North America, and is still in a good state of repair. For some time prior to its erection the congregation were permitted to worship in the old Roman Catholic Church belonging to the Recollet Fathers, which stood, until about two years ago, on the corner of Notre Dame and St. Helen-streets. This was kind of the Recollet Fathers, and it showed their wisdom. From that day to this the Catholics and Protestants of Montreal have lived together on the best of terms, and if occasional brawls have disturbed the streets, these have been caused by inconsiderate manifestations of over much zeal on the part of individuals, not from a sectarian spirit in the Churches. The Presbyterians of the time appreciated the courtesy of the priests, and in testimony of their gratitude presented them with a box of candles, 56 lbs., at 8d., and two hogsheads of Spanish wine containing 60 odd gallons each, amounting in all to £14.2.4. Mr. Bethune remained little more than a year in Montreal, and then removed to Williamstown, where he officiated till the day of his death, in 1815. Through his instrumentality churches were erected at Lancaster, Williamstown, Charlottenburgh, Martintown and Cornwall, in each of which he statedly preached. He was a man of great zeal and piety, deservedly esteemed by all who knew him, and whose name is still cherished in sacred remembrance by the descendants of those to whom he ministered. His remains lie interred in the grave-yard of Williamstown under a handsome monument that was erected to his memory by his six sons. Two of these sons took orders in the Church of England, and are still living, and both highly respected : the one, the very Reverend John Bethune, D.D., is Dean of Montreal; the other, the Right Reverend A. N. Bethune, D. D., &c., is Bishop of Toronto. The following extract from a letter of Dr. Mathieson's, dated April, 1864, has reference to the first Bishop of Toronto, the late Hon. and Right Rev. John Strachan, without doubt the most influential Scotchman who ever set foot in Canada, one who wielded more power in his day than any other individual in the Province did before or since, and whose noblest monument to-day, is the Church of England in the Province of Ontario. When he first joined it he was one of a mere handful of Anglican ministers. By sheer force of character he became their chief, and lived to witness his wide bishopric divided into three Sees with three hundred ministers, while he himself had conferred episcopal orders on no less than one hundred and sixty-six candidates. In giving the following passage the reader is asked to remember that the reference is to a time when Dr. Strachan swayed a political sceptre, when politics ran high, and when party feeling was strong. " It was in 1827 that our church began to be stirred into life. Dr. Strachan's famous ' Ecclesiastical Chart for the Province of Upper Canada' was one of the chief means of awakening it from slumber. His statements were manifestly so untrue as to require severe castigation : prose and poetry, ridicule and argument were pressed into the subject, and never was there such zeal displayed for the extension of our church and securing its legitimate privileges, unless it was when the late Mr. Hagerman made a rude attack on Scotchmen and their church in parliament, and aroused their indignation from Gaspé to Huron. Mr. Morris' mission to England was the result.

" Shortly after his arrival in this country Mr. Strachan wrote his two famous letters to, I think, Thomas Blackwood of Montreal, in which it was proposed that, if the St. Gabriel-street congregation, then the only Presbyterian Church in the city, would give him a good salary, he would return to Scotland for ordination and become their minister. *I have seen the letters.* A notarial copy of them was taken. The originals were in the possession of the late Mr. Ramsay, whose house took fire and many of his papers were burned. I once asked him if the Doctor's letters were saved; he gave no direct answer, but assured me there was a notarial copy of them. I inferred from the hints he gave that they were lost."

Let it not be supposed that the object in publishing this statement is to disparage the character of the Right Rev. prelate, deceased. He outlived all the *odium theologicum* which his chivalric zeal in support of his adopted church gave rise to. For him, personally, Dr. Mathieson frequently expressed his high admiration, nor could it be otherwise, for in many respects there was a very close resemblance of character in the two *bishops*. Great plainness of speech, indomitable perseverance, firmness, amounting at times to obstinacy, both possessed in a marked degree. It seems important, however, to establish a fact in connection with Dr. Strachan's early history, concerning which doubts have been expressed in certain quarters. In Mr. Fennings Taylor's ' Lives of the Last Three Bishops Appointed by the Crown for the Anglican Church of Canada " it is stated, page 193, " When Dr. Strachan arrived in Canada he had neither been confirmed by a bishop of his father's church, nor had he received the communion from a minister of his mother's church." His mother was a member of the Scottish Relief Denomination. " In fact he had by no religious act of his own become a member of any religious body."

It is difficult to reconcile this statement with that of Dr. Mathieson's, because, assuming that the letters spoken of were written by Mr Strachan, and we cannot conceive them to have been forgeries, there is strong presumptive evidence that Mr. Strachan must have studied theology at a Scottish University before coming to Canada, otherwise, he would not have spoken of going back "*for ordination.*" He could not receive ordination without going through the prescribed theological *curriculum.* Besides, the fact of his having been a Scottish parish school-master affords undoubted proof that he had connected himself with the Kirk of Scotland, for he could not be admitted to that office without signing the Confession of Faith and Formula of the Church of Scotland.* This *formula* is the same as is required to be signed by candidates for license to preach the Gospel, and could not be honestly signed by any one who was not a member of the Established Church. Thus it runs:—

I do hereby declare, that I do sincerely own and believe the whole doctrines contained in the Confession of Faith, approven by the General Assemblies of this National Church, and ratified by law in the year 1690, to be the truths of God : and I do own the same as the confession of my faith : as likewise, I do own the purity of worship presently authorized and practised in this church, and also the Presbyterian government and discipline now so happily established therein, and which, I am persuaded, are founded on the Word of God and agreeable thereto : and I promise that, through the grace of God, I shall firmly and constantly adhere to the same : and to the utmost of my power shall, in my station, assert, maintain and defend the said doctrine, worship, discipline and government of this church, by Kirk-sessions, Presbyteries, Provincial Synods, and General Assemblies : and that I shall in my practice, conform myself to the said worship, and submit to the said discipline and government, and never endeavour, directly or indirectly, the prejudice or subversion of the same : and I promise that I shall follow no divisive courses from the present establish-

---

* Cook's Styles, pp. 191 :—

ment in this church, renouncing all doctrines, tenets, and opinions whatsoever, contrary to, or inconsistent with, the said doctrine, worship, discipline, or government of this Church.

It is impossible to conceive of a more conscience-binding declaration than this, nor does the propriety of submitting any man, layman or cleric, to such a test obviously appear. It is surely better not to vow than to vow and not to pay; yet, this solemn vow has been broken in innumerable instances, and we know it will be broken again, by men who will strain at a gnat, and yet swallow a variety of camels. We have no quarrel with the Bishop for joining the Anglican Church, but rather with the despotic ecclesiasticism which weaves around men chains as complicated as the spider's airy web: and quite as weak. If it is needful to swear at all, the power that binds should have power to release, or, in some other mode, there should be devised a way of escape for all such as from conscientious motives wish to avail themselves of it. But this is by the way — our correspondent proceeds to say:—

"Doctor Spark I never saw; he was removed from his earthly labours before I came to the country. His widow, who afterwards married a Doctor Montgomerie, gave me several of his sermons in manuscript; from these, and the respect in which he was held by his people, the impression I have of him is that he was a man of considerable learning, inclined to literature, a correct writer, a grave divine, distinguished for his good sense more than originality, for his clear statements of truth more than the brilliant corruscations of genius. He was reported to be Arminian in his theology. He died suddenly on Sabbath afternoon, having preached in the forenoon from Genesis xiv, 24: "See that ye fall not out by the way," in which it was thought there were some coincident allusions to his untimely separation from his flock. If you can acquire a copy of the " Christian Examiner" for 1837 you will there find a valuable and ably written memoir of Doctor Spark, from the pen of his intimate friend, the late Doctor Daniel Wilkie of Quebec. He was succeeded in St. Andrew's Church, Quebec, by Doctor Harkness, in the year 1820. Harkness was for some time master in the Academy at Ayr; an open-hearted, generous fellow, but passionate and fearless, who often violated the rules of propriety and decorum when he was aroused. He was a great favourite with Lord Dalhousie, and a frequent guest at the Castle. His Lordship, while he was Governor General of Canada, visited Scotland in 1824, when I remember having met him, and heard him speak, with many eulogiums, of Harkness, but lamenting his fondness for card-playing and his passionate outbreaks. During his ministry in Quebec a burying-ground had been purchased by Protestants of all denominations, and, of the proprietors, I have been told, the Scotch were the most numerous. A pious fervour awoke the zeal of the Episcopalians; they thought it dreadful to lie in unconsecrated ground. The prospect of receiving the fees of interments perhaps animated the religious fervour of the clergy, and led them to apply to Sir James Kempt, then Governor General, for leave to consecrate the ground. Aware of what had occurred at Kingston, a short time before, Doctor Harkness was determined to preserve the rights of his people. About the consecration of the ground he was indifferent, but he would not allow fees to be exacted from the members of his congregation for the burial of their dead. Taking with him such documents as he thought necessary for the vindication of their claims, he went to the Castle, obtained an audience of the Governor, and laid before him the case, urging warmly His Excellency's acquiescence with his views. Sir James would not look through the same spectacles, but accused Harkness of bigotry and intolerance; the latter got angry and retorted bitterly and in uncourtly terms. The Governor felt insulted and rebuked the Doctor for his want of courtesy. Harkness shook his fist in his face, telling him he cared not for his approval and that he would carry the matter to the foot of the throne;' adding, you will not hear me, but *your master* will. The Aid-de camps alarmed, left the room, Harkness, gathering up his papers, put his hat, which he held in his hand, on his head. Indignant at his incivility Sir James said, ' Doctor Harkness, you might at least have been polite enough to have kept off your hat in my presence.' Off went the hat, and, bowing to the very ground, the Doctor replied, ' I will be as polite as you please, Sir James,' and, thrice repeating the action and the words, concluded with the caution,—' Take care what you do, I carry these papers to the foot of the throne.' Sir James, finding that he had got into an ignoble squabble, and being anxious to get out of it, asked the Doctor peremptorily what it was that he wanted. ' I have told you what you would not hear,' replied the enraged Doctor. ' They may consecrate their ground when they please. Presbyterians will sleep as sound in consecrated as in unconsecrated ground. *It's a' ane tae Dandy.* But nane o' them will mutter an ill-mumbled mass o'er a Presbyterian grave and ask twa dollars for the doin' o't.' The Doctor having then calmed down, condescended to explanations, which the Governor acknowledged to be reasonable. In a short time the matter was settled to the Doctor's satisfaction, and he withdrew with the bundle of papers under his arm, pointing to which, he addressed the astonished Aids as he passed out: 'Now, you can consecrate the ground when you like: I have got all that I want; our *rights* are secured.' And I believe the ground, notwithstanding the burning zeal of the time, remains unconsecrated till this day."

It has already been said that Dr. Mathieson was introduced to his charge in Montreal by the Rev. Archibald Connell of Martintown. Mr. Connell was a warm-hearted Highlander, then fresh from the heathery hills of Argyleshire, and, being of a frank and genial disposition, the Doctor and he soon became friends. But, sooner or later, the best of friends must part. Before ten years had gone round Dr. Mathieson was called upon to preach his friend's funeral sermon on the same day that he opened for worship the church of Martintown, which Mr. Connell had been instrumental in building. Upon a marble tablet on the church wall there is a touching allusion to the occasion, penned, there is reason to believe, by the Doctor; it reads as follows:—" Within this edifice, erected for the worship of God, his voice was only once heard proclaiming the tidings of salvation. Assembled with his flock under the open canopy of heaven, to show the Lord's death, they were driven by the inclemency of the day to seek shelter within its unfinished walls. By a remarkable coincidence, on that same day of the month—one year afterwards—his remains were interred on the very spot where he then stood to distribute the symbols of the Bread of Life, and by that solemn act, close his ministerial labours." Mr. Connell was buried beneath the pulpit. He was a man of genius, and in him was verified one of Shakespeare's many striking truisms that "Great wit is to madness near allied." He was so nervously excitable that his mind sometimes lost its balance, leaving in the minds of his friends serious apprehensions for the result. "Once," says Dr. Mathieson, "on a cold winter night he arrived at my house, from Martintown, wearied and faint from his journey and long fasting. He had eaten nothing the whole day, nor could we persuade him to take any food then. 'Make me a *bowl* of tea, and be sure you make it strong,' was his only request. It was procured, and, for a short time after he drank it, he raved like a maniac, and not till after he had slept for some hours were his words coherent. I have also been told that, after a long pedestrian excursion in Wales, he went to Liverpool, called for 'a bowl of strong tea,' fancied he was waylaid by enemies who sought his life, started for Scotland, and exhibited some fantastic tricks on board the steamer. On arriving at Glasgow he called a cab, drove straight to the college and detailed to the Professor of Divinity such a catalogue of horrors as nearly drove the worthy Doctor as crazy as he was himself. He was exceedingly fond of music, and played well on the *fiddle*. Once I remember, at Martintown, while playing a fine old Highland Lament, his eyes began to roll most fearfully, he seemed to gasp for breath, and I had to rise and stop his strains, which were too powerful for his sensitive mind to endure. A stranger one day, hearing him play, stepped unbidden into his room, complimented him on his skill, and requested 'a tune.' Connell laid down his fiddle, and called his servant to show '*the impudent intruder*' to the door. But he was a noble fellow whose like we have rarely seen."

Among the first proceedings of the Synod of 1831 a resolution was passed, requiring the several members of the Synod to prepare a report of the state of religion in their several congregations and neighbourhoods, and to transmit the same to the convener of the Committee on a Memorial to the General Assembly, with a view to their forwarding to Scotland detailed information respecting the spiritual destitution existing in Canada, and the consequent need of increased ministerial labour. A majority of the ministers complied with the mandate—some of them, *at their leisure*. The whole Presbytery of Glengary, however, Mr. Ketchan of Belleville, and Dr. Harkness of Quebec, having neglected to comply, were cited before the Synod and "suitably admonished." Dr. Mathieson, unwilling to be ranked as a recusant, transmitted a draft Report, reserving to himself the privilege of revising and elaborating it a future time. This he did, and, in due course prepared an exhaustive document which might have been entitled a topographical, statistical, commercial and ecclesiastical history of the Island of Montreal and adjacent parts, and to which was appended a succint history of the congregation of St. Andrew's Church, Montreal, which will form a fitting conclusion to this chapter of reminiscences.

HISTORY OF ST. ANDREW'S CHURCH, MONTREAL.

(Written in 1832.)

"The first authentic account of the congregation now forming the members of St. Andrew's Church, Montreal, which I have been able to obtain, is dated in November, 1804. I have been informed, however, that for six months before that time a number of individuals assembled for public worship in a large private room, under the pastoral care of the Rev. Robert Easton, who had been previously minister of a congregation in Hawick, * Roxburghshire, in connexion with the Associate Synod in Scotland. The papers relative to his settlement I have not seen, nor any authentic account of the probable number of the congregation at that period. I am inclined to believe that they were not properly organized as a religious body till the 2nd November, 1804. On that day the congregation met, pursuant to notice, and elected seventeen of their number to be a committee for managing their affairs. In January, 1805, a petition was presented in behalf of the congregation to the different branches of the Legislature, praying that their minister might be permitted to hold a legal register of the marriages, baptisms, and burials by him performed. This petition was refused at the time, but on what grounds I have not ascertained. Mr. Easton obtained registers in 1815. It had been the unceasing desire of the congregation from their formation, to get a suitable place erected for public worship, and, though the difficulties which presented themselves to this undertaking were formidable to a poor and a little flock, they determined that a vigorous effort should be made to accomplish their desire; accordingly, on the 1st February, 1805, a subscription was opened for that purpose. Their success was such as to give them every encouragement to proceed. Soon afterwards the committee appointed two of their number to look out for a suitable piece of ground for building a church, and were empowered to conclude a

* There is reason to believe that Mr. Easton came from the Town of Morpeth, instead of Hawick, as stated in the text.

purchase on behalf of the congregation. This sub-committee reported on the 10th of May that they had purchased two lots for the sum of £180, and an annuity on the joint lives of two ladies of £50, which was to be reduced to £37 10s. on the demise of one or either of them. One of the annuitants is still alive, (1832).

"One of these lots contained a good stone house, which has since fallen into such decay that it will require to be rebuilt before it can be tenantable; the other lot, being vacant, was reserved for building a church for the congregation. A few days after this purchase was concluded a series of resolutions were drawn up by the committee and a general meeting of the congregation called for the purpose of taking the same into consideration. When the committee of management was appointed it does not appear that their powers were defined, nor are there any instructions to them on record; but it is evident from the minutes that all matters of minor importance were transacted by their uncontrolled official power, while we must naturally infer, from the sanction of the congregation which was required to the above resolutions, that all matters of greater moment had to be approved by a majority of the whole congregation. By one of the aforesaid resolutions the congregation declared themselves to be 'in connection with the Associate Reformed Synod in Scotland, commonly called the Burgher Secession.' This act, however, was never homologated by that Reverend Body, and consequently fell to the ground. The resolutions were indeed presented to the Synod at a meeting held at Glasgow in 1806, together with a letter from the Elders and Managers of the Church craving to be taken into connection with the Synod, but nothing definite was done. The Synod delayed deciding on the said petition, and, meanwhile, appointed a committee of correspondence, who, it seems, never corresponded, and so the matter was lost sight of for nearly fifteen years. About 1820 a question arose how far, and in what manner, the congregation in Montreal stood connected with the said Associate Synod, and a reference was made to the Synod on the subject, but no entry was found in their minutes to show whether any decision had ever been come to in the matter.

" On the 15th October, 1805, the foundation stone of the church in St. Peter-street was laid, and the whole work finished in the beginning of April, 1807, at a cost of about £1500. The walls are substantially built. The dimensions are 70 by 51 feet, without: and, though a plain, it is a comfortable and commodious edifice and can contain with ease 760 persons. Galleries were erected in 1816 at an expense of £400, which was borrowed for the purpose.

" Mr. Easton's stipend, from the commencement of his ministerial labours in Montreal, was £125. In 1816 it was advanced to £200, and, in 1818, was further augmented to £250. In December, 1822, Mr. Easton proposed to resign his charge in consequence of the increasing infirmities of age and ill health, if a suitable provision was made for himself and his family. This was agreed to, and a resolution carried, that steps should be immediately taken to procure a minister of the established Church of Scotland ' *and none else.*' This being deemed too exclusive by many of the American members, they withdrew altogether from the church, built a separate place of worship, and have a minister from the United States. Eight or ten of the most respectable of the American families remained and are still in connection with the church, and I must in justice say that, in regard for our establishment, and attendance on divine ordinances, their conduct is truly exemplary.

"In accordance with the resolution above alluded to, a letter was addressed to the Rev. Drs. Chalmers and Dickson, and the late Mr. Andrew Thompson, empowering them to elect and send on an ordained minister to succeed Mr. Easton. This letter was accompanied with a bond for £200 currency *per annum*, as salary No reply having been received to this letter, another was dispatched on the 20th December, 1823, of similar import. Choice was soon afterwards made of Mr. John Burns, A.M., who was ordained by the Presbytery of Edinburgh, and arrived in Montreal on the fourth of July, 1824. Mr. Easton then formally resigned and retired on an annuity of £150, payable from the funds of the Church, which sum he continued to receive till his death, which took place in May, 1831. On the 9th July, 1824, the committee of arrangements, with the consent of the congregation, made an official declaration that they were 'christians in connexion with the established Church of Scotland, under the ministry of the Rev. John Burns,' to whom they promised all due obedience, encouragement and support in the Lord. This document, which is entered in the books of the committee of management and also of the session, may be considered as the basis of the present constitution of the Church which, however, is not very very definite. * About the same time

---

* At a meeting of the congregation held on the 12th of May, 1835, a well-digested constitution and code of laws was adopted for the management of its affairs. In 1849 the Congregation received an Act of Incorporation (12 Vict. Cap. 154). In the following year the constitution was revised and remodelled, and was adopted, in terms of the Act, on the

it was agreed to style the church and congregation by the name of St. Andrew's.

"Mr. Burns continued minister of St. Andrew's Church for nearly two years, when, having succeeded to some landed property in Scotland, he resigned his charge on the 10th of May, 1826, and returned to his native country. A congregational meeting was called to receive his resignation, when, in compliment to him for the fidelity with which he had laboured among them, they delegated to him power and authority to elect and send out a minister of the Church of Scotland to be their pastor. This power was accompanied with a bond for £250 salary. On the 25th September following, he appointed to the office Alexander Mathieson, A.M., a

---

11th March, 1851. It provides for an annual meeting of the congregation to be held on the 25th December, for the purpose of receiving a statement of all accounts and financial matters connected with the church. On the death or removal of the minister a meeting of the proprietors, pew-holders, and members of the church is convened, within eight days from the occurrence of the vacancy, when a committee of nine members in full communion is elected with full powers to take such steps as to them may seem best adapted for speedily obtaining a minister. By article I. of the constitution the congregation declare their adherence to the standards, form of worship, and government of the Church of Scotland. By the 18th Article the jurisdiction of the Synod of the Presbyterian Church of Canada in connection with the Church of Scotland is recognised. It being expressly understood, however, *that no act or declaration of the said Synod shall Contravene Article I. of these By-laws* The last article provides that every person, pew-holder or member, proprietor or sitter, shall subscribe the constitution before they can be competent to elect or be elected to any office.

licentiate of the Presbytery of Dumbarton, and residing within its bounds."

It is not necessary to continue the history of St. Andrew's congregation further than to state that, having greatly increased in numbers and in wealth, steps were taken in 1848 for the erection of a new church. The finest site in the city was secured, on the brow of Beaver Hall Hill, where was reared the finest specimen of ecclesiastical architecture hitherto attempted in Canada. The Cathedral of Salisbury, which is perhaps the most beautiful of its order in England, furnished the model from which Messrs. Tate and Smith, the architects, designed this admirable structure. They also superintended its construction, and e grafted, as it were, on this young colony hallowed associations and pleasing memories of the old world. The church was completed at a cost of about $64,000, and was opened for worship on the 12th of January, 1851.

On Saturday evening, the 23rd of October, 1869, the choir met in St. Andrew's Church as usual for practice. On their leaving, the customary precautions were observed in regard to the fires and gaslights, and by the time they had severally reached their homes a Sabbath's silence reigned in the streets of the city, unbroken, save by the howling of the wind, which blew in fitful gusts from the west.

In the gray dawn of the morning the great bell of the Cathedral tolled the alarm, and the wild cry of "Fire!" "fire!" awoke the citizens from their slumbers. Then there was a rushing to and fro of helmeted men, hasting to the rescue with reel and hose, with hook and ladder, each vying with the other to be the first at the scene of the conflagration, prepared to brave danger and death in their efforts to stay the devastation. But the devouring element had already the mastery. Soon the whole of the interior was consumed; the roof fell in with a tremendous crash; the insatiable flames shot up to the skies; they licked the gothic arches of the doors and windows; they enveloped the tall steeple as with a winding sheet of fire, and illumined the whole heavens with a lurid blaze of light. The Baptist Church, in the immediate vicinity, was several times in imminent danger, and was only saved from destruction by the heroic efforts of the fire brigade. The roof of the Universalist Church, immediately opposite, ignited, and was totally consumed. Many members of the congregation, who had been uninformed of the disaster, repaired on the Sabbath morning to "the place where prayer was wont to be made," and found it a mass of smoking ruins. Nothing remained of their "beautiful house" but the blackened walls. Fortunately for the congregation, the church was amply insured.

A costly and beautiful memorial window, which had been but two weeks before placed in the Church, in memory of the late Miss Mathieson, by the ladies of the congregation, perished in the general conflagration.

The revenues of St. Andrew's Church from pew rents, donations and weekly collections amounted in 1832 to £450. In 1869 the congregation contributed for all purposes connected with the church and college the sum of $14,036, a sufficient indication of their material prosperity. The general statistics of the congregation for the same years are, as nearly as can now be ascertained, as follows:

	1832.	1869.
Probable number of individuals belonging to the Congregation	1,500	1,300
Number on communion roll	250	500
Number of Sabbath-school scholars *	60	304
Number of Sabbath-school teachers	7	31
Amount of Stipend paid	250	3,600

There were in Montreal, in 1832, but two churches in connection with the Church of Scotland, embracing 3,144 souls. The corresponding numbers now are six churches and 4,477 adherents.

The population of the city when Dr. Mathieson arrived, in 1827, was 22,000. Now it is 150,000.

---

* Including the Bible Class.

CHAPTER EIGHTH.

DR. MATHIESON AS A MEMBER OF SYNOD.

By this time the reader has formed for himself at least a general and tolerably distinct idea of what sort of man Dr. Mathieson was in society, and as the minister of St. Andrew's congregation. He will have discovered the weak points of his character, at all events, no great pains have been taken to conceal them. *He must have looked with jaundiced eyes, or, through a distorted medium, who has not also found redeeming points in his nature sufficient to warrant him in saying :*

"He was a man, take him for all in all
I shall not look upon his like again."

In the Doctor's own words—already quoted as applied to another—"No man is all sinful or all holy, all morally base or truly great." The most luminous orb in the natural heavens, which dazzles and blinds the beholder with its brightness and glory, when subjected to the scrutinizing observation of the physicist is seen to have spots on its surface, and, while human nature remains as at present constituted, we shall never want proof that man was made " a little lower than the angels."

To present a faithful picture of Dr. Mathieson as a member of the Synod, to describe his appearances, to define his principles of church polity, to estimate the influence which he exerted upon others, has from the commencement of this sketch been regarded by us as that to which should be attached the highest value, and in a proportionate degree has this part of the work loomed out in the distance, great, difficult, almost unapproachable. To be true to nature, the brain that conceives the portraiture must be clearer and more fertile, the hand that wields the brush must be steadier and more skilful than his whose chief part in these preceding pages has been the easy and congenial task of selecting and culling the flowers that lay thickly strewn around his path. But that from which we thus confessedly had shrunk, another has done for us, and this estimate of the Doctor's character is the more valuable that it comes from a clergyman who did not always agree with the Doctor in the church courts, and who not unfrequently fell under his lash. Without note, comment, or reservation, we thankfully accept this opportune contribution, and endorse every word of it—premising only that our good friend in his prefatory remarks, overlooked the fact that what he modestly pleads as an apology for his impromptu letter was precisely the kind of mental discipline that he stood in need of.

"I know no one who courted popularity, for its own sake, less than Dr. Mathieson did. Of course, like all men, he loved power and influence, but he would never condescend to acquire it by trimming his sails to the popular breeze. He was too outspoken, and cared too little to conciliate those who were opposed to him in opinion, to have his name associated with triumphant votes. Hence he was more frequently counted with the minority.

"No face was more radiant than his, however, when he felt that he was in sympathy with the Synod, as a whole; as for instance, always, when reading and commenting upon the annual report of the Widows' Fund, his smile was most benignant, and his eye was filled with kindly warmth. The same was true of his treatment of all persons who were in accord with his views—when at any time they addressed the Synod. It was really a temptation to one to coincide with him—even against better judgment and conviction—to obtain a hearty recognition from him. But woe to him that roused the Doctor's wrath! And this was not hard to do. Let the slightest symptom of departure from what he thought the constitutional principles and practice of the Church of Scotland be shown and the Doctor's agitated countenance and restless attitude became quite a study. He seemed like a proud steed held in check with the bridle—'champing his iron curb.' Very frequently he would not wait until the speaker sat down to express his protest against anything that seemed to him in the remotest way to argue contempt of, or indifference to, the parent church; but would interrupt him in spite of all rules and cries of 'order!' And, when he rose in such circumstances, the hearts of common disputants quailed before him. His lips firmly compressed, betokening the resolution of his nature, indignation seated on his brow, and his eyes flashing forth scornful fire—particularly if the opponent happened to be in the Doctor's estimation, *young and inexperienced, and therefore presumptuous*—this was enough to bear the unlucky wight to the ground; so that it mattered not that the Doctor did not find free utterance. Like the full bottle, the few words that came out of his lips in spurts, being clenched by the determined force with which the staff was brought to the ground, were more powerfully eloquent and effective than full flowing periods decked out in the ordinary dress of rhetoric, but which want the subjective reality and earnestness that characterized the Doctor.

"Dr. Mathieson did not shine in debate. He was governed in his views more by instinct and feeling rather than by a strict acquiescence with the laws and requirements of the Church of Canada, and thus had to speak everything that occurred to him, when it did so occur, whether it was *in order* to do so or not, sometimes rising half a dozen times in a single debate. Nevertheless he was very influential, though not possessing the qualities needful in a leader. His personal presence and bearing were much in his favour—men of meaner exterior felt themselves at a disadvantage when arrayed in opposition to him. Of late years, too, the remembrance of his long and faithful services added weight to his views, while his well-known loyalty to the church gave him a hold on the sympathies of all who had a spark of chivalry in their nature, so that even those whom he took to task in no honeyed words could not help respecting him as an earnest, honest man. It cannot be doubted that all through our church's history his views helped to mould the legislation of the church if they did not control it—giving to it a conservative tone; so that on the whole, the Synod was the arena on which he appeared to greatest advantage."

To the above apposite and comprehensive sketch we have nothing to add, and it only remains to glean from the minutes of Synod a few of the more prominent subjects of discussion that arose in the church during the thirty-eight years in which Doctor Mathieson was a member of the Court. During that time we venture to say that no one man ever approached him in the number of dissents, protests and appeals entered in his name. In fact, he was never known to submit to an adverse vote upon an important question without insisting on this *privilege*, which was usually recorded in this way. "Against this decision Mr. Alexander Mathieson entered his dissent for reasons to be given in due time, taking instruments in the clerk's hands and craving extracts." This "taking instruments" simply means the handing the clerk the sum of one shilling for every protest taken, a part which the Doctor used to perform with great *gusto*, and with such a pressure of the *thumb* as almost to leave the impress of the coin on the table. "Craving extracts" implies a demand for a copy of such part of the proceedings as may be asked for, and which is furnished on payment of the usual fee.

Whether it was the case of an individual minister or of a body of ministers belonging to another denomination that knocked at the door of the Kirk in Canada, seeking admittance, it seemed to be the Doctor's peculiar prerogative to make sure that their declaration of adherence to the Confession of Faith and Formula lacked nothing of the minutest punctilio. If it were a minister of the Church of Scotland who had come to Canada asking to be "received" he was met on the threshold by the Doctor, insisting upon a sight of his "Presbyterial certificate." In this regard the Doctor was not exceeded by the old parish minister, who emphatically declared that he would not have allowed the Apostle Paul himself to preach in *his* pulpit " until he had produced his Presbyterial certificate." It has already been said that at the time of the formation of our Synod, in 1831, there existed in Canada a body of Presbyterians, known as the "United Synod of Upper Canada," composed chiefly of seceders. Negotiations were early commenced with a view to their joining the Synod in connection with the Church of Scotland. By reason of the opposition, however, of the party who acknowledged Doctor Mathieson as their leader and mouth-piece this union was delayed until the year 1840, when, in amendment to the resolution to receive the members of the said Synod, it was moved by Doctor Mathieson that a committee be appointed to confer with the United Synod and to report on the evidence laid before them of the ministerial character, the literary acquirements, *and the soundness in the faith* of these dissenting brethren, &c., &c. After long reasoning the motion was carried by thirty-five, to three, Doctor Mathieson as usual entering his dissent, "for reasons then given in, and for other reasons which he may give in in due time." It is but right to add that the satisfaction of having done "his duty" was sufficient to console the Doctor under such circumstances, and that his subsequent intercourse with the brethren was always kindly and courteous.

It was in 1834 that Doctor Mathieson overtured the Synod to take into consideration the propriety of establishing public schools in Canada after the manner and pattern of the Scottish parochial schools, but, if the proposal was seriously entertained by the Synod at the time, it does not appear to have led to any practical results. From the year 1831 up to 1840 the adjustment of the Clergy Reserves of Canada was the *quæstio vexata* which occupied by far the largest portion of the time and deliberations of the Synod.

DR. MATHIESON AS A MEMBER OF SYNOD.   125

This was a subject that afforded Doctor Mathieson full scope for displaying to good advantage the determination and indomitable perseverance of his nature. It was not a favour that his Church was seeking—it was " a right" that was to be *demanded* and, if need be, fought for to the death. Although the chief credit must be awarded to the late Hon. William Morris for the ultimate recognition of the claims of this Church to an equal share in the Reserves with the Church of England, upon the ground that in terms of the treaty of union between England and Scotland the one Colonial Church had as good a right to be designated an Established Church as the other, there can be no doubt that Doctor Mathieson's unwearied efforts were largely conducive to the settlement of the question. The correspondence which during these years he maintained with the Earl of Durham, Lord Glenelg, Sir George Grey and other officials of Her Majesty's Imperial Government, as well as with the Governors General of Canada, would of itself fill a volume, and sufficiently attest the Doctor's claim on the gratitude of the whole church. The only *fee*, however, that the Doctor received for these services, so far as we know, was the honourable, but somewhat onerous, appointment to a seat on the Board for the management of the Fund which his energy had been instrumental in creating; a position that he held till the close of his life, and to the duties of which he always applied himself with exemplary zeal and fidelity.

That period in the history of the Church commonly known as " the Disruption," and which culminated in 1844 by the withdrawal of twenty-four ministers who at that time declared their sympathies with the Free Protesting Church of Scotland, and erected themselves into a separate communion, was the cause of a painful and life-long regret to the Doctor, who never could forgive " the Frees" for their defection from the *Auld Mother Kirk* which he himself loved so well.

The disruption of the Church of Canada followed, as an inevitable consequence, the disruption in Scotland. There are those who maintain that whatever cause there was for the division that took place in Scotland there was none in Canada. If patronage was a grievance there, it never existed in Canada. If it was wrong for the civil power to intermeddle with ecclesiastic polity, or interfere with its jurisdiction, such exercise of the secular prerogative was unknown in Canada. Why should a church thus happily free from these creative elements of discord seek to be mixed up in a quarrel not of their own making, and to make sacrifices for principles which could have no bearing on their own practice and procedures? After a lapse of six and twenty years it is easy and natural to argue after that fashion, but the fallacy involved is none the less apparent. "*Cœlum non animum mutant qui trans mare currunt.**" When it shall become a law of nature for a mother to forget her child, or the child its mother, then will the withholding of sympathy be accounted a virtue. The disruption in Canada was purely a matter of sympathy, the avowal of which, on either hand, became tantamount to an espousal of the cause. If we say it was uncalled for, we stultify the men who were the chief actors in it, and that we do not wish to do. More than that, we can afford now, to say, " it was all for the best." But these were

---

* They who cross the sea change their sky but not their affections.

stormy days in the Synod, from the third to the tenth of July, 1844, when it was sought to define the relations that did, or *should*, exist been the Presbyterian Church in Canada and the Church of Scotland. By some it was thought a division would be obviated, without the compromise of principle, by simply dropping the words, from the designation of the Church, " *in connection with the Church of Scotland.*" Doctor Mathieson would never consent to *that*, but gave in a *protest*, on behalf of himself and certain others, to the effect " that their taking part in the discussion should not be held as an admission on their part that such discussion was not in its nature *unconstitutional, incompetent,* or *ultra vires*, and, in particular, that their so taking part and voting should not invalidate their right to remain and continue to be the Synod of the Presbyterian Church of Canada, *in connection with the Church of Scotland*, and to enjoy all the privileges belonging to the same. The Doctor's sentiments prevailed, and without having altered its designation the Synod adjourned, to meet again on the 18th of September, which day it accordingly met, *minus* the nineteen ministers and eighteen elders who had given their adherence to the protest and dissent of Mr. Bayne, of Galt, who had previously moved a resolution that the obnoxious words should be struck out, and that the Church, thenceforth, should be designated *the Presbyterian Church of Canada*.

In all the subsequent missionary and benevolent operations of the church, Doctor Mathieson's counsels and co-operation were sought and freely tendered. He was the principal promoter, and, for many years, the active convener of the French Mission Committee. He was a member of the committee for the management of the Ministers' Widows' and Orphans' Fund from its commencement, and was its chairman and guiding spirit as long as he lived. At the foundation of Queen's College, in 1840, Doctor Mathieson was among the first to be named a trustee, and, during the thirty years in which he was a member of the Board, no one was more regular in attending its meetings, nor more earnest in promoting the best interests of the College. In consequence of the unhappy suit in the Court of Chancery which followed the removal of a professor from the College, in 1864, Doctor Mathieson's name obtained a wide celebrity, during several years, in law circles, both as defendant and plaintiff, in the actions of " Wier *versus* Mathieson," and " Mathieson *versus* Wier," the several pleadings and judgments in which were regarded by the profession with peculiar interest, as involving an important precedent in determining whether the professor's tenure of office was, *ad vitam aut culpam*, or, during the pleasure only of those who appointed him. The decree of Chancery affirmed that the professor had been improperly " removed," and that the trustees consenting thereto were personally liable for the costs incurred in the case. In May, 1865, Doctor Mathieson thus refers to the decision: " you have heard the decree of Chancery amercing individuals in costs, Doctor Urquhart and I have resolved to go to jail rather than submit to such an iniquitous judgment. I have no hope that our appeal on the main question will be successful, whatever be the after proceedings; but, that a body of men, gratuitously discharging an important duty and acting from the conscientious conviction of saving the Institution from ruin, and' without a particle of ill-will to the dismissed, should be thus dealt with is an outrageous violation of common sense ; but I hope we shall all at least be "Merry Martyrs." In the Court of Error and Appeal, to which the case was carried, the decree was reversed, and the Doctor became jubilant as the visions of prison doors and grated windows vanished from his imagination.

There was no duty ever assigned to Dr. Mathieson that he discharged with more satisfaction to himself and credit to the Church than the visit which he paid to the churches in the Maritime Provinces, as a delegate from the Canadian Synod, in the year 1855. He returned from that visit impressed with the depth and solemnity of the piety that pervaded the various congregations with which he was brought into contact, and which reminded him of the religious character of the rural parishes of his loved native land. From an admirable report* of the intercourse he then had with the brethren of Nova Scotia the following extract may be given :—

"Your deputation met with the kindest reception from the lay members of the congregations of Halifax, and, indeed, wherever they went, while the Synod welcomed them with joy, as a prelude to more frequent intercourse and co-operation, and invited them to take seats as members of the court, and a part in all its deliberations, after having expressed in the warmest terms, through the Moderator, 'gratitude to the Church of Scotland in Canada for having sent a deputation of their number to them, and to the members of the deputation themselves for executing the commission, and coming from so great a distance to visit them.' Having sojourned a few days at Halifax we proceeded to Pictou, staying one day at Truro, around which the country spreads out in fertile

---

* Synod Minutes of, 1856, pp. 45, 53.

vales, watered by fine streams. On Sabbath the pulpit at Pictou was supplied by Mr. McKid, and at Roger's Hill by Dr. Mathieson. Large and attentive audiences were assembled in both places. In the evening Dr. Mathieson preached to a large congregation in the Rev. Mr. Bain's church, reciprocating the kind feelings with which your deputation was invariably received by their United Presbyterian brethren ; on Monday, took part in a very interesting missionary meeting in Mr. Bain's Church, and listened with much pleasure to the interesting details of their Mission in New Hebrides ; on Tuesday we visited New Glasgow, where the Rev. Allan Pollok is settled over a large and flourishing congregation. It is hardly possible to speak in too strong terms of the earnest missionary spirit, of their devotedness to their work, and the eminent success of the young ministers that have been recently sent from Scotland to fill the deserted pulpits of Nova Scotia. Snodgrass, Sprott, McKay, Pollok, McLean, and Herdman, are names that will be remembered as zealous preachers of the Gospel of salvation, long after they shall have passed away from the scenes of their labours.

" In the afternoon we visited Mr. McGillivray, of McLennan's Mountain. At the time of the Schism in 1843, he, only, ' faithful among many faithless, found.' Several ministers left their charges for more lucrative appointments in Scotland, or joined the Free Church. Their deserted people were like sheep without a shepherd, Mr. McGillivray alone remaining to watch for their spiritual interests, and plead the cause of the Church of Scotland....... On one occasion, both the scene and the circumstances were of the most interesting nature, one of your deputation, being engaged to assist at the dispensation of the Lord's Supper, had nearly thirty miles to travel, he accordingly gave instructions that the person who was to convey him to the ground should come at nine o'clock A.M., but, instead of that hour, he came at six, and every moment was impatient to start. We set out at half-past nine at a rapid trot, and having driven a considerable distance, found a relay of horses, that greater speed might be obtained. Ignorant of the driver's purpose, he was frequently exhorted to slacken rein; but the only reply was *we will be late*, and another admonition to the noble animal to renewed speed. At length the mystery of our rapid flight was unveiled. About three o'clock P.M. we came to a beautiful sylvan spot where we found a congregation of from 1500 to 2000, listening with profound attention to ' *the men*' who, one after another, at the call of their minister, addressed the people on the topic which had been announced for discussion in the morning. The congregation took little notice of our arrival, but observed the same riveted attention to the speakers. Not a movement was made, nor a sound heard but the wind among the trees, and the voice of the speaker echoing through the deep forest—a voice which in prayer was empassioned fervour, chastened into tones of reverence and deep humility. And the Psalm, Oh that Psalm! as it rose, in wild irregular notes, from two thousand voices, it struck home to our hearts and christian sympathies with a power that can never be forgotten. It was now five in the afternoon, and thus had it been with them since eleven in the morning. Previous to our witnessing this interesting spectacle we confess to having cherished a rooted prejudice against such systematized lay instructions, as being fraught with danger to the peace of congregations and conducive to spiritual pride; but we cannot help thinking that such patriarchs as *these* are invaluable helps to the Christian Ministry. In after conversation we found them to be men of the right stamp.... The same devotional stillness and decorum characterized all the days of their solemnities, and on the Sabbath, as the symbols of the Bread of Life were spread out on rude planks, covered over with linen of snowy whiteness, and surrounded by blooming youth and gray-haired pilgrims, may we not hope that that green spot in the forest was but a type of a greener spot in the vale of life, where the pilgrims to the heavenly Jerusalem shall rest and find themselves refreshed from the wells of salvation... We also learned that many young men might be found here of a true spirit, who might be induced to enter on a course of preparatory study for the Ministry. Indeed, we were impressed with the conviction that it is from Nova Scotia that we must look for the supply of Gaelic-speaking students. The specimens you already have in Queen's College do credit to their country and their church." The recollection of this tour in the Lower Provinces was a theme on which the Doctor ever delighted to dwell, and he has been heard to remark, that in all his journeys he was accompanied by his most valued friend, Mr. William Edmonstone, " who displayed a reverend zeal in the cause, and was apparently as anxious about getting good ministers, and making suitable provision for them, as he was for the proper equipment of his ships." This pilgrimage continued till the last to be a green spot in the Doctor's memory.

But the most characteristic of all Doctor Mathieson's appearances as a member of the Synod remains to be told. In 1860 it had become known that these British North American colonies were to be honoured by a visit from His Royal Highness the Prince of Wales, and everywhere preparations were set on foot for giving him a right loyal and hearty welcome. The Synod of the Church of Scotland must join with other corporations in presenting through its Moderator an address; and who so well fitted as " the father of the Church" to be spokesman on the august occasion! Doctor Mathieson was already an ex-Moderator. He had been elevated to that dignity in 1832, and, though the procedure was an exceptional one, he was now reinvested with the highest office which it was in the power of the Synod to bestow, and, with him, Dr. Cook, Dr. Barclay, the Clerk, Messrs. John Greenshields and Alexander Morris, were appointed a committee to make all the necessary arrangements for the presentation of the address. The Governor General was informed by letter that the Synod had prepared an address to His Royal Highness, and information was asked for in regard to the arrangements that would be allowed for its presentation, and the hope expressed that the ministers and elders might be invited to be present. The reply of the Governor's Secretary contained these words: " The address to His Royal Highness should be presented at one of the levees which he will hold during his visit to Canada." A copy of the address was next forwarded to the Governor's Secretary along with the intimation that the committee would be glad to receive further instructions for their guidance. " I presume," was the Secretary's reply, " that the Synod of the Presbyterian Church of Canada may select any of the places named in the *Gazette* of August the 4th at which levees will be held for the presentation of addresses." Montreal was one of the places so named, and it was resolved that the address should be presented there. But as to the particular time and formalities to be observed, the committee were kept in profound and perplexing ignorance. The only information they felt warranted in making to the members of the Synod was, that the address would *probably* be presented in Montreal on Monday, the 27th instant. A few days after the circulation of this notice, it was generally understood that the levee would be held in the afternoon of the 29th. It was therefore supposed that the committee might safely call a meeting of ministers and elders to be held in St. Andrew's Church *at noon* of that day. A notice to that effect was accordingly issued on the 21st of August. Meanwhile the Synod clerk, Mr. Snodgrass, did his best to get an audience of the Governor's Secretary, between his arrival in Montreal and the 27th August, if possible, to obtain more definite information as to the course of procedure likely to be followed.

On making enquiry at the St. Lawrence Hall, he was told that "the Governor's Secretary *was taking his tea.*" He wrote him a letter, but was coolly informed that no answer would be given that night (Saturday, the 24th.) To make matters worse, it was now made public that the levee was to begin at *eleven* o'clock, forenoon, instead of in the afternoon as formerly announced By this time the Moderator had become prodigiously indignant over the muddelling unsatisfactory nature of the negotiations, and, accompanied by Dr. Barclay, proceeded in person to the hotel, and demanded an interview of the Provincial Secretary, Colonel Irvine. He was courteously received, but learned nothing definite respecting the presentation of the address, but, from the conversation, was led to suppose that it would be presented in the same manner and at the same time as that of the Church of England. The reply of the Governor's Secretary to the clerk of Synod's letter of Saturday evening was put into Dr. Mathieson's hand as he was departing: it was to the effect that the number of addresses being so great, and the pressure such, there would not be time *to read them* at the levee, but that the bearer of each address, on being presented to his Royal Highness, should hand to the Prince the address with which he was charged, and pass on, and that written answers would subsequently be sent to all addresses presented. After reading this letter the two Doctors in Divinity were put to a stand as to how they should act in the case. In passing along the hall of the hotel, they opportunely met Mr. Pennifather, the Secretary, and entered into conversation with him on the subject. He candidly admitted that he had foreseen the difficulty that was likely to arise, but saw no way of counteracting it. He knew that there was no answer prepared. Dr. Barclay immediately put to him the question, whether the address from the Church of England was to be read in presence of His Royal Highness, and he replied, he believed it was: when the Moderator said,—"under these circumstances that from the Church of Scotland could not be presented." The situation had now become a most embarrassing one. There was not a moment to be lost. Immediately it was resolved to address a letter to His Grace the Duke of Newcastle, of which the following is a copy, and such of the members of the committee as were nigh were hastily convened:

"MONTREAL, 27th August, 1860.

"MY LORD DUKE,—

"I have dutifully to acknowledge the receipt, through the Governor General's Secretary, of the notification, that it is His Royal Highness' pleasure to receive the address of the Church of Scotland from myself as the bearer of it, but not to be read or replied to at the time. Having been informed that a different course is to be followed in the reception of the address from the sister Church of England, I beg very respectfully to represent to your Grace, that, as a branch of the established Churches of the Empire, the Church of Scotland in Canada is, in the eye of the law, constitutionally on a footing of equality with the Church of England in this Province, and that whatever privileges are possessed by the one church belong of right to the other.

"Of course, as individuals, the members of the deputation are proud of the opportunity of expressing, in any way that may be pointed out to them, their loyalty to the Crown and their respect for His Royal Highness, but, as representing the Church of Scotland in Canada, their consenting to occupy a position of inferiority to that accorded to the sister Church of England, on so interesting an occasion as the present, would be received with extreme suspicion by the large and respectable body on whose behalf they have been appointed to act.

"I would moreover respectfully represent that the address is that of the Synod of the whole Church in Canada, and that ministers and elders from various parts of the Province are in attendance for the purpose of presenting the same.

"Respectfully requesting a consideration of the statements of this letter,
"I have the honour to be, &c., &c.,
"ALEXANDER MATHIESON, D.D.,
"Moderator."

The draft of this letter was submitted to the committee of Synod, which met at ten o'clock, and the course proposed was adopted by the majority of those present. Others were disposed to regard the whole matter as an insult to the Church of Scotland, and would enter into no further negotiations. The draft was adopted, however, and having been engrossed, was put into the hands of His Grace so soon as he entered the appartments where the levee was to be held, in the hope that, even then, it might be possible to obtain, at least, a verbal reply. What a hurrying to and fro there was that morning!—Of country ministers in search of gowns and bands — of elders, imploring the loan of courtly garments they had never donned before. Having been one of the party, the writer can testify to the excitement that prevailed as the representatives of the Kirk collectively wended their way to the Court House, headed by their Moderator, of portly aspect, and venerable mien, mingled with the throng of two thousand citizens that were congregated there, and endured all the tortures of an unmitigated squeeze, preparatory to their being ushered into the Royal presence. The denouement was at hand. The Judges and Roman Catholic Clergy were first received; the Anglican Bishop and Synod followed; the deputation from the Synod of the Church of Scotland was then called for presentation, and entered the presence, still uncertain as to the fate of their address. Would it be read and replied to ? The odds were against it. The Moderator, in full court dress, advanced, saluted the Prince, and was about to retire when he was asked by the Earl of St. Germain if he had an address, and answered in the affirmative. Under an impression that this was a command to present it in the same manner as had just been done by the Bishop of the Church of England, the Moderator unrolled his parchment and was in the act of commencing to read it when Sir Edmund Head, the Governor General, came forward and said the address was not to be read, but simply put into the Prince's hand, and that an answer would be duly returned. The Moderator informed him that such a course would neither be satisfactory to the Deputation nor respectful to their church, and that under such circumstance, he must decline presenting it at all. So saying, with rare presence of mind and dignity, he rolled the parchment up, handed it to the Clerk of Synod, was presented to His Royal Highness, made a profound bow, and withdrew. While the other members of the Deputation were making their bows it was whispered into the Moderator's ear that the Duke of Newcastle desired him to wait on him after the levee. The levee being over His Grace entered into conversation with the Moderator, expressed regret for the *contretemps*, and endeavoured to mollify matters by explaining that, owing to the large number of addresses, all could not be read; that the Free Church might demand the same privilege, and that a line must be drawn somewhere. The Moderator replied that in his opinion the line had been drawn where it ought not to have been drawn- between the established churches of the Empire, which stood equal in the eye of the law. That the Free Church stood in a different relation to the State, and that, in his opinion, as well as in their own, the distinction was sufficiently wide. The Duke replied, you must be aware that there are no established churches in this Province. The Moderator said he was aware of the fact, and was sorry for the sake of true religion that it was so, adding his opinion, that the members of the Established Churches of England and Scotland had certain rights and privileges in every part of the Empire, wherever they might be found.. The interview terminated by the Duke's assuring the Moderator that he should hear farther from him in regard to the address. A meeting of the Synod's Committee was forthwith held, when it was resolved to address another letter to the Duke of Newcastle setting forth the position of the Church in Canada, and defending the course which the Moderator had been constrained to take. A short extract must suffice, for the present, from the long letter that was immediately dispatched to His Grace.

" It will, I am persuaded, be with feelings of deepest pain that the members of the Church of Scotland will learn that an address from the Synod of their Church in Canada, was not permitted to be read to His Royal Highness, when addresses from two *local* Synods of the Church of England, in Quebec and Montreal, were formally presented and specially replied to. And this the more, that twenty years ago the question of the relative rights of the two Churches was understood to have been finally set at rest, in accordance with the claims of the adherents of the Church of Scotland which were based upon the Act of Union between England and Scotland; the decision of the twelve Judges of England having affirmed the equality of the Church of Scotland in Canada with the

Church of England. The revival of a question so long disposed of is deeply to be deplored, but yet I feel I would be wanting in my duty were I not again to solicit, as I now do, that an audience should be granted for the purpose of presenting our address on terms of equality with the sister Church of England, at such time and place as His Royal Highness shall be pleased to appoint, &c., &c."

In the meantime the Moderator and several members of the Deputation, personally, received warm expressions of sympathy from the Lord Bishop of Montreal and many of his clergy. He also received His Excellency the Governor General's commands to dine with the Prince of Wales on Wednesday the 29th, when he had the honour of shaking hands with His Royal Highness, and could not refrain from breathing an audible prayer for his welfare. Explanations of a highly satisfactory nature followed, and an understanding was arrived at that the address would be received, and replied to, at Kingston, which might be regarded as the most appropriate place for its presentation, being the city from whence it was dated, and being the seat of the college of our Church. A correspondent, who was present on the occasion, has kindly furnished the following sketch of the proceedings at Kingston, on Tuesday, the 5th of September:

"Doctor Mathieson, as Moderator, attended by a number of ministers and elders were in readiness to present the Synod's Address to His Royal Highness. So soon as definite intelligence reached the party that there was no prospect of the Prince's landing at Kingston, they prepared to go on board the steamer containing H. R. H. which lay at anchor in the inner harbour. For this purpose the representatives of the Synod moved from the City Buildings, in which they had met, to the wharf, where a tender was in waiting to convey the party to the steamer. The procession, as it passed through the masses of human beings that lined the street bordering on the water, was a source of wonderment to the on-lookers. As they gazed on the majestic figure of the leader with cocked hat and in full court dress, with gown covering all, followed by his robed attendants, they evidently were puzzled to make out who we were. How proud we all were of our grand old Coryphœus! All eyes were fixed on him. Arrived on board the "Kingston," we were conducted to the saloon, and at once found ourselves in the Royal presence. Having arranged ourselves in front of the Prince and party, the *famous* address was handed to the Doctor, who, with leisurely self-composure, unrolled the document, and proceeded to read it. The whole Doctor was in the reading There was dignity, courtly breeding, and loyal respect in every tone. So soon as it was read, and the Prince had made his reply thereto, the party were presented in order, when, however, the *formal* proceedings were ended, the Prince stepped forward, stretched out his right hand, and said: "Doctor Mathieson, allow me to do myself the pleasure of shaking hands with you." The tear started to the Doctor's eye; and throwing warmest blood into his fingers, he grasped the royal hand with a right Scottish grip, while the loyalty of his big heart rushed to his lips in the irresistable utterance: ' *God bless you!* ' "

At the following meeting of the Synod Doctor Mathieson read the narrative of proceedings connected with the presentation of the Synod's address from which these notes have been chiefly derived, when it was unanimously resolved, " that this Court express, and hereby expresses, its entire satisfaction with the dignified conduct of Doctor Mathieson on that occasion.*

Our biography would be incomplete without some allusion to Doctor Mathieson's views on the *Union Question.* That was a subject which was never mentioned in his hearing without calling forth a very strong expression of opinion, and we have not to travel very far for a reason. It was not to be expected that one, who had all his lifetime been so demonstrative in his attachment to the Church of Scotland, who prided himself so much on his personal connection with it, and had battled so strongly for its principles and privileges, would be likely to regard with much favour any proposal by which the relationship might be weakened or jeopardized, or, that would commit him to any policy whereby his loyalty to the Parent Church could possibly be called in question. Others might speak of connection with the Church of Scotland as a matter of small importance—as a mere myth—a romantic hallucination. Not so the Doctor. In *his* estimation it was a sacred bond, to sever which were sacrilege, and, as he could not conceive of any basis of union with other Presbyterian Churches that would not ask him to renounce allegiance to the Church he loved so well, therefore, he instinctively set his seal of disapprobation on every proposal that involved even a discussion of the question. It was not that he was uncharitable or intolerant, narrow-minded or bigoted. No one ever charged him with being influenced by such unworthy and unchristian motives. On the contrary, those who

---

* A copy of the address is to be found in the printed minutes of the Synod for 1860, page 73.

differed most widely from him on this question never doubted that he was thoroughly honest and consistent in the matter. On its own merits, he did not choose to argue the case; but when forced to do so, he defended his opinions with great *vim*, if not always very logically.

The union question was only twice brought formally before the Synod. The first occasion was by an overture introduced by Doctor George " on a union between this church and other Presbyterian churches in this Province." This was in 1860, and, the Doctor being Moderator, had of course to waive his right to *protest*, and it must be held to be remarkable that in his closing address, in which the proceedings of the Synod are generally reviewed in detail and discanted upon, he did not suffer the slightest allusion to the question to escape him. His mind seems to have been surcharged on that occasion with a sense of the responsibilities belonging to the ministerial office, and in the concluding sentences of his address he pressed these upon the attention of his brethren with great earnestness : " You are now about to return to your houses, your families, your flocks, and to engage again in the great work to which the measures that have been taken by Synod are only subservient. Your special work is to preach the Gospel of the Lord Jesus Christ, and to diffuse, a pure, a healthy, and enlightened religion throughout the land. *This* is the most important work that can be committed to you, and your responsibility in the execution of this work is in proportion to its excellency. Let this conviction be an abiding principle of your conduct. Cherish it. Act upon it; and you will be drawn from all dependence upon yourselves to lay hold on the arm of Him who can sustain you.

Well might you tremble in consideration of the magnitude of the work, and, in view of the interests you are called to promote, you might well exclaim with the Apostle to the Gentiles, who is sufficient for these things?...... But though a minister has his trials, peculiar to himself, he has also his joys, with which 'a stranger intermeddleth not.' These sustain and support him amidst many hours of weakness and fatiguing thought. And he has One, mightier than all others, ever near him, to strengthen and encourage him. Endeavour to realize His promise, ' Lo, I am with you always.' Take courage, brethren, and go forth to the discharge of your duties in His sustaining strength. Think of His exalted nature, on the greatness of His work, on the intensity of His love for man, for those whom He has committed to your special care. Endeavour to have a just sense of the honour He has conferred on you in making you ' fellow-workers with Himself in bringing many sons into glory.' These reflections will animate you with the purest zeal and the highest christian motives. Animated by love, and sustained by constant, fervent prayer, you will go forth to your work with alacrity, you will prosecute it earnestly, and you will be rewarded by seeing the work of the Lord prospering in your hands. Brethren, to God and the word of His grace I commend you."

In 1866 the union question again came before the Synod, which met in Toronto, by overture from the Presbytery of Ottawa, " anent an union between this church and the Canada Presbyterian church," when twenty-three voted that the overture should lie upon the table of the Synod until the next annual meeting, and thirty-three that it be rejected. In explanation of the wording of the original motion and the smallness of the vote, it may be mentioned that the attendance was unusually small that year on account of the Fenian invasion that had spread consternation through the Province a few days before the meeting of the Synod. Such was the state of excitement in the country, it was generally supposed that the meeting of the Synod would have been postponed. The whole country was up in arms—from Montreal to Toronto the frontier bristled with bayonets. A whole fleet of steamboats, hastily extemporized into gunboats, patrolled the waters of the St. Lawrence and the lakes. The quiet old town of Cornwall suddenly found its population doubled—two thousand volunteers, representing every arm of the service, were quartered on its inhabitants, while its principal streets were barricaded with Armstrong guns. Such a sight had never been seen before in Canada. In the neighbourhood of Prescott the spectacle was such as none who witnessed it can ever forget. The sloping banks were white with military tents, the wharves were crowded by armed men— volunteers from Perth and Pakenham and other places far in the interior—splendid looking fellows, many of whom had never seen the St. Lawrence before. The shore was lined with gunboats. On the opposite side of the river, too, around Ogdensburgh, could be descried the long straight lines of tented soldiery and the low dark hulls of vessels of war at anchor, with steam up, guarding the harbour, not from a dreaded attack of the British, but to aid in protecting Canadians from the lawless bands of ruffians who were plotting treason on American soil, and seeking to embroil the United States Government in war with their peaceable and unoffending neighbours. And so it was at every important point along the route, while such of the inhabitants as were not under arms were busying

T

Well might you tremble in consideration of the magnitude of the work, and, in view of the interests you are called to promote, you might well exclaim with the Apostle to the Gentiles, who is sufficient for these things?...... But though a minister has his trials, peculiar to himself, he has also his joys, with which 'a stranger intermeddleth not.' These sustain and support him amidst many hours of weakness and fatiguing thought. And he has One, mightier than all others, ever near him, to strengthen and encourage him. Endeavour to realize His promise, ' Lo, I am with you always.' Take courage, brethren, and go forth to the discharge of your duties in His sustaining strength. Think of His exalted nature, on the greatness of His work, on the intensity of His love for man, for those whom He has committed to your special care. Endeavour to have a just sense of the honour He has conferred on you in making you 'fellow-workers with Himself in bringing many sons into glory.' These reflections will animate you with the purest zeal and the highest christian motives. Animated by love, and sustained by constant, fervent prayer, you will go forth to your work with alacrity, you will prosecute it earnestly, and you will be rewarded by seeing the work of the Lord prospering in your hands. Brethren, to God and the word of His grace I commend you."

In 1866 the union question again came before the Synod, which met in Toronto, by overture from the Presbytery of Ottawa, " anent an union between this church and the Canada Presbyterian church," when twenty-three voted that the overture should lie upon the table of the Synod until the next annual meeting, and thirty three that it be rejected. In explanation of the wording of the original motion and the smallness of the vote, it may be mentioned that the attendance was unusually small that year on account of the Fenian invasion that had spread consternation through the Province a few days before the meeting of the Synod. Such was the state of excitement in the country, it was generally supposed that the meeting of the Synod would have been postponed. The whole country was up in arms—from Montreal to Toronto the frontier bristled with bayonets. A whole fleet of steamboats, hastily extemporized into gunboats, patrolled the waters of the St. Lawrence and the lakes. The quiet old town of Cornwall suddenly found its population doubled—two thousand volunteers, representing every arm of the service, were quartered on its inhabitants, while its principal streets were barricaded with Armstrong guns. Such a sight had never been seen before in Canada. In the neighbourhood of Prescott the spectacle was such as none who witnessed it can ever forget. The sloping banks were white with military tents, the wharves were crowded by armed men— volunteers from Perth and Pakenham and other places far in the interior—splendid looking fellows, many of whom had never seen the St. Lawrence before. The shore was lined with gunboats. On the opposite side of the river, too, around Ogdensburgh, could be descried the long straight lines of tented soldiery and the low dark hulls of vessels of war at anchor, with steam up, guarding the harbour, not from a dreaded attack of the British, but to aid in protecting Canadians from the lawless bands of ruffians who were plotting treason on American soil, and seeking to embroil the United States Government in war with their peaceable and unoffending neighbours. And so it was at every important point along the route, while such of the inhabitants as were not under arms were busying with great apprehension. The impracticability of the thing renders it almost ridiculous. The mischief that would involve our churches, the unsettlement of the rights of property with the renunciation of the name, the lawsuits that would follow, the bitterness and contentions that would arise out of it, are alarming. But I need not vex myself on the subject. I will not be long a combatant in defence of honoured rights. And I have been given to understand that the movement was only abandoned till a few of the *old fogies* had quitted the field—out of pure compassion to them!—poor, prejudiced, hirpling creatures, who cannot keep up with the intellectual march of the times! and that *then* both Synods should memorialize their respective Assemblies, crave permission to renounce all denominational names, rights and privileges, shake hands, get the Parliament to sanction the measure, when peace and quietness would be expected to reign!"

"The headlong spirit of the times" to which the Doctor here alludes had probably reference to the discussion then being carried on in Scotland about "innovations," so called, under which heading, we suppose, is comprehended every several departure from "the book of our Common Order, and the Directory for the Public Worship of God," which was adopted by the Church of Scotland and ratified by the Scottish Parliament so long ago as the year 1645. From another letter we learn the Doctor's mind on the matter. "The Assembly's measures may be stringent, more so, perhaps, than would be necessary were the Church in a sound state of thinking on matters of doctrine and government. But when, according to newspaper reports, we hear Dr. McLeod declaring that the fourth commandment was abrogated by the ristian economy, and Lee, Tulloch, and Story, &c., advocating measures subversive of the distinctive characteristics of Presbyterianism, Pirie's motion was not too strong. The innovations of old Grey Friars (Lee's Church) is, I am informed, incipient Popery,* and I am inclined to believe it. Such changes as the progress of the age and taste of the times demand, and that could safely be introduced, might be adopted; but the innovating party, in contempt of the *honest* prejudices or piety of the people, have forced their opinions so as to awaken a just alarm for the safety of true church principles. Favourable as I am to instrumental music as an aid to congregational psalmody, or, even, as I might be to a well-digested liturgy, as a help to poor spiritless drones, I do not wish that they should supplant the fervour either of real devotional feeling or drown the tones of the sweet human voice. Story has sent me a copy of his Report, '(of the Church Service Society it is presumed).' I am one of the Old School, and c'ing to the forms that

---

* It may be right to inform such of our readers as are not familiar with the topics here alluded to that Dr. Lee's "Popery" went no farther than making use of a printed form of prayer, composed by himself, in public worship, and in teaching his congregation to stand while singing the praises of God, and to kneel in prayer. If we remember rightly, Dr. Lee also admitted to having, upon a certain occasion, administered the communion to an aged sick person *in private*. He had likewise accustomed his congregation to say *Amen* after the prayer. For these he was adjudged to be an "innovator" by the Presbytery of Edinburgh, and also by the Synod of Lothian and Tweed-dale, upon which Dr. Lee appealed to the Assembly, and, after a long and exciting contest, he won the day. This discussion is set forth at large in "The Life and Remains of Robert Lee D.D.," by the Rev. R. H. Story, recently published.

have done more for Scotland than any new-fangled nostrums will ever accomplish for her. The piety of the people has been cherished and sustained by the good sense, deep thought, and godly feelings of her ministers. As these qualities decay, somewhat of the Lee, Tulloch, or Story school may be brought in with seeming advantage for a time, but I am afraid that with such forms the people in this age will get formal too."

So much for Dr. Mathieson's colloquial treatment of the union question. It is but fair now to quote a few sentences from his sermon preached before the Synod in 1861 wherein his graver thoughts on this important subject are very clearly and emphatically set forth,—" It appears to be necessary to the full development of the Christian Church, that there be divisions in the visible body, so that those whose faith and practice are approved by God, may be made manifest. But though divisions are wisely permitted and over-ruled for the general good of the Church, and every attempt that has hitherto been made to gather into one community the discordant and repellant elements of humanity, has utterly failed; are we to encourage religious dissensions, and sanction the bitter strifes and animosities that flow out of them? Far from it: we deplore ecclesiastical dissensions as an enormous evil,—an evil that impedes the progress of genuine Christianity—that exhausts the energies of the Church, in internicene strife—that neutralizes the principles of true Christian fellowship, and puts to an almost hopeless distance, the prospect of the Universal Church ' walking by the same rule and minding the same thing.' Although there be little scriptural unity now, it is attainable, but progressive. The great business of the Church is to edify the body of Christ, 'till we all come to the unity of the faith, and of the knowledge of the Son of God, unto a perfect man, unto the measure of the Stature of the fulness of Christ.' Even in external forms and ceremonies, union is an object most desirable—an object to be kept constantly in view, and its attainment aimed at, in the pure spirit of brotherly love.'

During the last three years of his life a very marked change was observable in Dr. Mathieson's Synod appearances. It was not altogether that he had lost the fire of youth. Certainly it was not that his mental faculties were greatly impaired; these retained their force and freshness, in a remarkable degree, to the very last. But he felt himself physically incapacitated for taking an active part in the proceedings of the Synod; he had no longer the agility of former years by which to spring to his feet, as of yore, and put a stop to " the drivellings " of some luckless speaker who imagined he was electrifying his audience, but whose arguments in the Doctor's estimation, were " *perfect nonsense.*" It was with difficulty he could rise at all. His old enemy, rheumatism, had stiffened his joints, and the disease that ultimately carried him to the grave had fastened on him. He began to realize that his synodical career and his earthly existence were soon to terminate, that THE night was coming, in which none can work. And it does not admit of a doubt that, gradually, as he neared the shores of " the better country," things of time and sense paled before his vision; that considerations to which he had once attached importance receded from his view; that his mind became more solemnly impressed with the paramount importance of those Christian truths which he had so often preached to others; and that he became more deeply sensible of his own need of "that Holiness without which no man shall see the Lord." He knew that he had often done the things that he ought not to have done, and left undone the things which he ought to have done; that he had said things that he ought not to have said; and though he was not the man to make a parade of his religious convictions before his fellow-men, he did not seek to dissemble nor cloak them before the face of his Heavenly Father. He could say with St. Paul; "Brethren, I count not myself to have apprehended; but this one thing I do, forgetting those things which are behind, and reaching forth unto those things which are before, I press toward the mark for the prize of the high calling of God in Christ Jesus." "We are troubled on every side, yet not distressed: We are perplexed, but not in despair." Had he been pressed to give an exposition of his faith and hope, he would have said no more than this, "By the Grace of God, I am, what I am."

The Synod which met in Kingston in 1868 was distinguished by the harmony which pervaded its deliberations. It was also distinguished for an unprecedented manifestation of catholicity on the part of its members. The conference of the Wesleyan Methodist Church was simultaneously assembled in the same city, and it was resolved, without a dissentient voice, that a deputation should be sent to the conference to convey to its members the christian greetings of the Church of Scotland in Canada. It were easy to imagine that Dr. Mathieson might have objected to the proposal, on constitutional grounds, as being opposed to the use and wont of the Church of Scotland to acknowledge or recognize "dissent" in any form. Had he regarded the proposition as a matter of mere policy or expediency he would have set his face against it, and frowned it down. The time was when he would have done so. But, believing, as he *now* did, that there was involved no compromise of principle, and that the expression of good will intended to be conveyed was honest and sincere, he would not forbid the banns; and in that large assemblage that met in St. Andrew's Church to receive the addresses in reply from the Methodist brethren there was no face that beamed with more evident satisfaction than that of the old Doctor, nor heart that throbbed with nobler impulses than his, nor voice that sang with deeper pathos the familiar lines:

> " Behold how good a thing it is,
> And how becoming well,
> Together such as brethren are
> In unity to dwell."

What shall we say of the Synod that met in Hamilton in the following year, 1869 ? What *can* be said, to make it more memorable, than that it was the last meeting of the Synod at which the noble form of the now venerable minister of St. Andrew's Church, Montreal, was seen ? This can be said: that Dr. Mathieson was selected by the Moderator to preach on the morning of the sabbath, and that it was the subject of general remark, that, if ever the Doctor exceeded himself, it was on this occasion. His sermon was remarkable for freshness of thought, for earnestness and grace of delivery, for, indeed, all that constitutes power in preaching. Again, this meeting of Synod is memorable for the interchange of cordial brotherly salutation, with the brethren of the Canada Presbyterian Church—a manifestation of Christian fellowship which the Doctor did not attempt to suppress, but which, on the contrary, met his hearty approval, shewing conclusively that he was not the uncompromising, vindictive opponent to union, which some supposed. Lastly, that it was marked by a solemnity unknown in all the previous history of the Synod. It was fitting that Dr. Mathieson should close his connection with the Supreme Court of his church with a sacredness becoming the occasion. Often had these ministers placed in the hands of the people committed to their charge the memorials of Redeeming Love. Often had they adressed to others the words: "This do in remembrance of Me"; but never before, as a body of ministers, representing a branch of the Christian Church, had they themselves surrounded the Table of their Lord and Master. Such an observance of the Holy Sacrament by the Synod was without precedent in the Courts of the Church of Scotland. In former years Dr. Mathieson might have had doubts as to the suitableness of the ceremonial to the occasion, but he had none now. At that Communion Table we reverently take leave of our loved friend and father, as a member of Synod. Let imagination fill up the picture. Let memory imprint it on the mind never to be effaced,

> "Till death-divided friends at last
> Shall meet, to part no more."

CHAPTER NINTH.

NOTICE OF DR. MATHIESON'S DEATH AND FUNERAL, EXTRACTS FROM "THE PRESBYTERIAN" AND OTHER SOURCES.

Some extracts from a biographical notice hastily prepared for "the Presbyterian," shortly after Dr. Mathieson's death, will form a suitable continuation and conclusion of these memoirs, and may be helpful to the reader in forming a general estimate of that character of which we have been endeavouring to delineate a few separate and distinct traits.

Seldom has it devolved upon any journalist to record the death of one who, in his life-time, enjoyed more largely the respect of his fellow-men than did the subject of this notice, the late Minister of Saint Andrew's Church, Montreal, who departed this life on Monday morning, the 14th of February, in the 75th year of his age, and the forty-fourth of his ministry in this city. Although our departed friend and father had thus passed the usual limits of man's age; yet his admirably developed physique, his robust constitution, his regularity of life, and the mental vigour retained by him to the last, were all such as justified the expectation that he might have attained a still greater longevity; and even he himself has been heard to express the hope that he would reach the years of his father, who died at the age of eighty-two. Nevertheless it may be said that he has gone down to the grave in a good old age, full of years and full of honour; and, what concerns us vastly more, full of faith in the doctrines of Christianity which he had so long preached to others, and full of assured hope for the life to come. We know that this humble tribute to his memory has been anticipated by others, and it accords better with our present feelings that we are found reflecting the public opinion, rather than seeking to form it. By the death of Dr. Mathieson, the City of Montreal has lost a good citizen, and society a distinguished ornament. Others will doubtless be found to enter upon those beneficent labours from which he has ceased. Another minister will supply the pulpit of Saint Andrew's Church; another member will occupy his seat at the Councils of the Temporalities' Board; another Trustee will be elected for Queen's College; another manager for the Ministers' Widows' and Orphans' Fund; another patron will be found for the St. Andrew's Home; but there is a sense in which *his* place will not and cannot be filled. His removal from us is the disappearance of an old familiar land-mark, his separation from us, the severance of a link connecting the present with the past history of the country and the Church, that cannot be repaired. In looking back through the vista of years during which our late friend lived and laboured among us, if it is difficult to realize that changes so great and so varied should have transpired during a single life-time, it is no less difficult to form a correct estimate of the influence exerted upon a community by a Christian Minister, who, during all these years of unexampled progress and prosperity, occupied a prominent and an honourable position. In 1826, when Mr. Mathieson first took up his residence in Montreal, the city wore an aspect, scarcely a single feature of which can be recognized at the present time. Few cities in the world have undergone so thorough a transformation in so short a period. Then, it was an unimportant town, little more than an outport of Quebec, without wharves, without shipping, without manufactures, and without those means of communication that have made it what it is. Then, it had a population of probably not more than 22,000, and of these the English-speaking inhabitants formed scarcely an appreciable minority. Now, it is the commercial capital of British North America, the centre and seat of wealth, intelligence and enterprise. Its population has risen to 150,000, while recent statistics have brought to light the significant fact that the assessed value of the property held by Protestants is largely in excess of that held by the Roman Catholic population.

In speaking of the character of the venerable minister now gone from us, we love to think of a man endowed with many noble qualities, yet a man, subject to like passions and infirmities as we are, differing chiefly from others in the intenseness which marked the characteristics of his nature. In outward aspect he was of fine personal appearance and of commanding presence, courtly and dignified in his bearing, but not ostentatious. Observing the strictest propriety of costume at all times, he showed not only his sense of self-respect, but manifested also a becoming regard for the ministerial office, a duty which, by precept as well as by his own example, he omitted no opportunity of impressing upon others. No one could be long in his company without feeling that he was in the presence of a gentleman, a man of superior intelligence, of acute observation, and of large information. Not only was he an accomplished scholar; he kept abreast of modern thought and literature, and he was conversant with the great questions of the day. Had you looked in upon him during the eventful crises of the Italian revolution, of the Indian mutiny, the Crimean war, or the Abyssinian expedition, you would have found him reading the best authenticated histories of these countries, studying with minute interest their geography, and acquainting himself with the physiological peculiarities of their inhabitants. He was a great reader, and, although unknown in the world of letters, was a voluminous writer, of which his written sermons alone, not to speak of his other manuscripts, furnish marked evidence; for, whether we regard the depth of thought, the beauty and diversity of imagery, the chasteness of language, or the general carefulness of composition, these will compare favourably with the writings of the most gifted men. He was never known to preach an extempore sermon, and during those frequent excursions which in his earlier days he made into the country, where he found neither churches nor pulpits to preach in, his ingenuity was often taxed to supply the indispensable reading desk. An instance of this occurred in 1828, at Huntingdon, then a county town consisting of six or seven houses, where he had received a warm welcome from one of the people, who gathered the neighbours and requested the Doctor to address them. "Being *a paper reader*," as he himself describes it, "I had to erect a pulpit by the fireside, which was easily extemporized by two chairs, back to back, and a four legged stool laid across and covered over by a piece of carpet." Of the amount of labour he underwent in visiting the settlements in the valley of the Chateauguay, at a time when they were wholly destitute of the stated ordinances of religion, it is impossible now to form an adequate conception; but in spite of the difficulties he encountered in the shape of bad roads, or rather the want of roads and of conveyances, to the end of his life he referred to these excursions, as associated with the happiest of his memories. In the year already mentioned he had been asked to go into the country, thirty miles or so, to officiate at a marriage, and he thus describes the only mode of travelling then available: "At Caughnawaga, I found myself among the Red Indians in want of a guide and a conveyance to take me through the six miles of forest and tangled brush I had to traverse, but how to make my wants known I knew not. All my jerks and gestures failed to convey my meaning, till a youth took up the idea of a man on horse-back, which he endeavoured to imitate, who, on receiving an expression of my satisfaction, went off in an instant, and returned, leading by the mane a shaggy pony whose bones were too angular for bareback riding. At length a saddle was procured with only one stirrup—we supplied the other with a rope—and an iron bit having been found, with a new hempen cord we made a bridle. I was hoisted into the saddle with my valise lashed behind, and my *Registers*, two quarto volumes of considerable size—under my arm. My red guide, whose dress consisted of a pair of linen drawers and moccasins, kept up with the trot of the pony, admonishing it betimes to a quicker pace with the willow branch which he carried in his hand.

Through the dense forest, sometimes almost brushed off by the branches, we hastened along the rough path, and in less than an hour emerged on a settlement on the Chateauguay." These illustrations of preaching and travelling under difficulties, recall to mind disabilities of another kind that sound strange to our ears. Up to the date of these incidents, and indeed, for a number of years afterwards, no marriage in the Province was accounted legal unless the Clergyman celebrating it had obtained permission to keep a Register, previously paraphed by one of the Prothonotaries of His Majesty's Court of King's Bench, and as permission to keep such records was confined to a very small number of ministers of the Established Churches, it followed that a great many marriages and baptisms performed by the representatives of other religious denominations were in the eye of the law null and void. It must be supposed that subsequent legislation came to the relief of these early settlers, but at all events it is certain that Dr. Mathieson was not unfrequently called upon to remarry parties who, after many years of married life, had made the unpleasant discovery that they were living in doubtful wedlock. In respect of baptism, the Doctor often found himself at a loss how to proceed. He was too good a a Presbyterian to dispense this privilege without being satisfied that the lives of the applicants were, outwardly at least, in accordance with their own baptismal vows. It frequently happened that at the close of a service in a private house or school-room, a dozen or more children were brought to him for baptism. To use his own language on one of these occasions:—" The parties were unknown to me; what was I to do ? Admit them indiscriminately, or institute an enquiry into their character and christian knowledge ?

For that there was no time, and I might be imposed upon. I immediately, in the presence of the congregation, commanded my elder, to whom the people were all well known, to select two discreet and pious men, and this being done, I addressed them, enjoining them to recommend those parents only whom they in their conscience considered worthy to have their children admitted to the ordinance On this being done, I laid a solemn injunction on them in regard to their parental duties. This part of the service was interesting and impressive, and my good elder complimented me on my address, saying, that if I would speak as well *without the paper* at home, I would soon attach to me the whole community." It was indeed a very singular trait in the Doctor's ministerial character, that while he felt himself on ordinary occasions utterly and constitutionally unfitted to appear before an audience without his manuscript, in presiding over a communion table, and administering the ordinance of baptism, there were few to compare with him in the fluency and power which characterized his addresses.

The law allowed the officiating minister to exact the fee of five shillings for every registration of baptism, but the Doctor invariably refused to receive a penny, thinking it "horrible to sell a christian ordinance." Upon one occasion the elected elders withheld their consent to the application of a drunken father who wanted baptism for his child; the man became furious and even threatened to thresh the minister into compliance, but the Doctor remained inexorable. It having been stated to him, however, that the mother of the child was a good pious woman, upon her he put the vows in the presence of her husband, and with such allusion to his conduct as brought tears to his eyes, and drew from him an humble apology, with the promise that he would become a better man.

These are mere passing allusions to the Doctor's early ministerial career. Though in themselves trifling, they give us a glimpse of the joyous and yet earnest spirit which animated him even in the discharge of irksome duty. It were easy to fill a volume with such reminiscences of his life, and it is to be hoped that some one of his many intimate friends will undertake the preparation of an extended biography for which we believe there is abundant material existing. To have known Dr. Mathieson, as an intimate friend, was indeed a great privilege, for he was the truest of friends. The shadow of suspicion as to the sincerity of his professions could never for one moment be entertained. He was outspoken in stating his opinions, and none the less, though his dearest friends should be the subject of remark; and while at times he spoke perhaps too strongly, he ever spoke and acted under an honest conviction of the truth and justice of the principles he maintained. Policy and expediency were terms wholly unknown in his vocabulary and, he regarded them as " simply intolerable " in others.

Had it not been for this conspicuous trait in his character his influence in the Synod and other Church Courts would have been overwhelming. He was too diffident, however, to excel in debate, and too uncompromising in the maintenance of his opinions, even when great principles were not at stake, ever to become a party leader; and the respect, amounting to veneration, which was accorded him by nearly all his brother ministers, was traceable to his personal qualities as a man, to his moral worth, and to his loyalty and devotion to the Church. We have heard it said of

SUMMARY OF HIS CHARACTER. 163

him, that "it was impossible for him to conceive a meanness." We may add that he abhorred the very appearance of meanness in another. That he was twice chosen moderator of the Synod—an exceptional procedure in the practice of the Church—was of itself a high testimony of confidence reposed in him. The first occasion was in the year 1832, and following so soon after the formation of the Court, shewed that at that early period he had already made his mark. The second instance was even more noticeable, because it singled him out as the most fitting representative of the Church of Scotland in Canada, upon whom should be devolved the duty and high honour of presenting the Synod's address of congratulation and welcome to the Prince of Wales when he visited the British North American possessions in 1860; and the characteristic dignity and presence of mind with which he vindicated the honour of his Church upon that occasion, will not soon be forgotten.

As might have been expected from one in whom a stern sense of duty so largely predominated, Dr. Mathieson was regular in his attendance upon Church Courts. During the whole course of his ministry he was not absent from the meeting of Synod upon more than three or four occasions, and then, he was either out of the country or prevented by indisposition from attending.

But while the Doctor gave much time and thought and valuable assistance to the general business of the Church, it was in a special manner as the minister of St. Andrew's Church, that he desired, above all else, his services to be known and appreciated. Of his preaching before his own congregation we need not say more than that it was able, earnest, practical, and scriptural, and that it was a faithful reflection of the doctrines of the Westminster Confession.

He delighted to set forth the unity of the Divine procedure in the government of the universe, not distinguishing Providence from Grace, as though they were separate domains, but recognizing Redemption as an integral part of the comprehensive control exercised by the Creator over all his works. He dwelt also with special emphasis upon the necessity of *personal regeneration* by the Divine Spirit. Time and space would fail us to speak of his ministrations by the bedsides of the sick and the dying. The paternal regard that he had for the poor of his parish bordered almost on romance. How he visited them in their humble abodes! How he sat down at the end of every year with one or more of his elders and rigidly scrutinized the demands of every claimant upon the bounty of the session! How much discrimination he observed in dispensing the charities which the accumulated Church collections, added to the gifts of private friends, had placed at his disposal!

But perhaps the noblest trait of his disposition, one liable to mis-interpretation, was that which irresistibly prompted him to sympathize with the misfortunes of the unfortunate. Whether it was the case of one unjustly stigmatized by an unfeeling world, or whether it was that of a weak brother who had yielded to temptation, no appeal was ever made to him for aid or comfort in vain. To stand by a friend in need; to shield him from obloquy; to relieve him from present want; to defend him, if he could; to mitigate, if it were possible, a deserved punishment; to bring up again such an one to a position of usefulness and respectability, that was the highest gratification which he could propose to himself. It was not that he connived at the fault; but, against the principle of keeping a man down who had inadvertently fallen, he invariably protested.

For about ten years preceding his death, the rheumatic attacks to which he had been occasionally subject, became more frequent and severe. An asthmatic affection, with which he had also been sometimes troubled, grew upon him with advancing years. More recently, having suffered at invervals from irregular action of the heart, it became necessary for him to intrust his late worthy and able assistant and successor, Mr. Paton, with the burden of the pastoral work. It was not, however, till the dispensation of the communion in October last, upon which occasion he preached and presided, that the state of his health became a matter of solicitude to his friends. He was advised by his medical attendant to abstain altogether from pulpit duties, and although he did so for a time, he yielded to the strong desire which he had to preach to his congregation on the last Sabbath of the year, the same sermon that he preached that day forty-three years before — his first Sabbath in Montreal.

The last occasion on which he preached was on Sabbath, the 23rd of January, three weeks before his death, when he spoke for fifty-five minutes from the text. " It was winter. "

The effort was too much for him. He felt seriously unwell the next day, and for several days after, but he rallied sufficiently to take a short drive on the following Thursday. On Friday, the 28th, " the old Doctor " was seen in the streets of Montreal for the last time. A little group of friends gathered round his sleigh at the Post Office, where he had halted to mail his last letters for Scotland. Few were the words spoken, but the ominous looks of one and another told that the pale ensign of death was seen to be stealing over his forehead. The picture then imprinted on memory was not that of a noble ship wrecked on a foreign strand, but, rather, of a dismantled man of war, riding quietly at anchor, in safe moorings—the last round of ammunition expended, the battle fought and won—the colours still nailed to the mast—awaiting orders to be refitted. And as he took leave of us, and directed his course by the old familiar way, imagination overheard the parting soliloquy,—Farewell crowded thoroughfare! Farewell city of palaces! Farewell dear old St. Andrew's Church, beautiful in thy ruins! Farewell to wealth, pomp, fashion: to ambition, applause and fame! To earth farewell! " I have a building of God, an house not made with hands, eternal in the heavens."

After this there came two weeks of great bodily weakness and severe suffering, of mortal conflict with the last enemy; two weeks during which love and friendship, kindred and acquaintance waited upon him with tenderest regard, and during which he daily received, with inexpressible satisfaction, the consolations of religion at the hands of a brother minister. Then came "the messenger of Peace that calls the soul to Heaven."

The funeral took place from his late residence in City Councillors-street, on the Thursday following, when a large concourse assembled within and without the dwelling. Soon after the appointed hour the funeral cortege was formed and proceeded to St Paul's, which had been placed at the disposal of the Trustees of St. Andrew's Church. The order of procession was as follows: The hearse, with four ministers and four elders, as pall-bearers, walking on either side. There immediately followed the hearse, Dr. Mathieson's two sons and the numerous connections of the family. Then came the Moderator and the Clerk of Synod, dressed in their robes, followed by the clergy of the Presbytery of Montreal, and by a number of the clergy of other denominations. After these, the elders of other congregations, members of St. Andrew's congregation, the St. Andrew's Society, and a large representation of all classes of the community. On arriving at the Church, the coffin, literally covered with exquisite flowers, was placed in front of the pulpit, which, together with the screen of the choir, was appropriately draped in black cloth, giving to the whole scene a very solemn and impressive effect. Every part of the capacious and beautiful structure was filled, and amongst the many that were observed to be present was the venerable minister of Cornwall, the Reverend Dr. Urquhart, who is the only clerical contemporary of the deceased now living. The ministers of the Montreal Presbytery present were Dr. Muir, Dr. Jenkins, Messrs. Simpson, McDonald, Sym, Patterson, Masson, Thomas Fraser, Joshua Fraser, Donald Ross, B.D., Campbell, Barr, and Black; Queen's College was represented by the very Rev. Principal Snodgrass and Professor McKerras; Toronto Presbytery, by the Rev. Kenneth McLennan; and that of Quebec by the Rev. Mr. Tanner of Sherbrooke. Among the ministers of other denominations present were noticed Dr. De Sola, the Jewish Rabbi, the Rev. John Cordner, Rev. Canon Bancroft, Canon Balch, Dr. Taylor, Dr. Wilkes, Mr. Ellegood, Mr. Dumoulin, Mr. Carmichael and Mr. Gibson, together with several others whose names we did not learn.

The services were conducted in a very impressive manner by the Rev. Dr. Jenkins. After repeating the Lord's prayer, four verses of the 53rd paraphrase were sung, commencing with the lines:

> "Take comfort, Christians, when your friends
> In Jesus fall asleep:
> Their better being never ends;
> Why then dejected weep?"

These verses were sung to the plaintive tune of "Comfort." The last line, "Why then dejected weep?" being repeated at the end of each verse, produced an effect very touching and in perfect harmony with the occasion. The singing was led by the organist and choir of St. Andrew's congregation. Suitable portions of Scripture from both the Testaments having been read, an eloquent and appropriate funeral address was delivered by the presiding minister, in substance as follows:

ADDRESS.

Fathers, Brethren, and Friends.

I might well shrink from undertaking the solemn task which falls to me to day, and lay upon others this sad service of love and regard for the venerable man whose remains we are bearing to the tomb; the more, because there are here ministers who have known him during nearly the whole course of his official career. The position which I hold in the Church, however, and the daily intercourse which I have enjoyed with our departed brother during the last three weeks, have led to my being pressed into a service, which, I may say, could be performed by no one who entertains a deeper reverence than I do for his noble, upright character.

This is not the occasion for presenting a detailed history of the life and work of the late minister of St. Andrew's Church, or for sketching the features, intellectual and moral, which so strongly characterized him. This is an office which will be discharged by others, I trust, at a more fitting time. To day, rather let us seize upon the few thoughts which these solemn scenes suggest, and make such personal application of them as may tend to our comfort and improvement. Let us see whether we cannot become better ministers, better Christians, better men, by the part we take in this burial.

Death, in this instance, has severed many a tie. The parental tie is severed, and the children of our friend are driven to look to Him who " in His holy habitation " is " a Father of the fatherless." On their behalf we also cast our eye heavenward, and upward send our prayers for their comfort, their guidance, their salvation. The tie of friendship is broken. For who can doubt that, during the residence of such a man for forty years in one place, there were formed friendships of the firmest and tenderest character. The pastoral tie is rent. How strong that tie becomes through the growth of years you know who have seen this venerable minister go in and out among you for almost two generations. The Presbyterial tie is sundered. We, his co-presbyters, are called to mourn the loss of the father of our Presbytery, the father, indeed, of our church in this country. Much might we say of him in these several relations: of his faithfulness, of his courage, of his self-denying work when he was left almost alone in our Church here, of his journeyings oft, of his perils, of his anxious care of the churches, of his faithful counsels in sickness and sorrow, of his

w

consideration, almost to a fault, for the failings of others, of his tenderness in seeking to restore those who were overtaken in error or sin, of the faithful nature of his friendships, of his generousness to the poor, of the comforting and hope-inspiring words with which he was ever ready to sustain the hearts of the dying. Not that we would set him forth as faultless! Those lips, now closed in death, would reprove us, could they be but opened, were we for one moment to attempt the concealment of frailties and imperfections which our brother consciously shared with us all, and which are the common heritage of our now fallen humanity. What we do say is that in him whose remains lie before us, we have lost much that was valuable to us all, whether in the family, in the congregation, or in the Church at large, that in him were qualities of strength, of firmness, of endurance, of courage, of self-forgetfulness and of faith, upon the like of which we shall seldom, if ever, look again. Had he lived in the days when the Covenanters laid down their lives for their principles, he would have been among the first of Scottish martyrs. In these characteristics he has left to his children, and to his brethren in Christ's ministry, a noble legacy which they will do well sacredly to hold and cherish.

He is gone! We shall see no more that noble form! We shall not again hear his voice giving utterance to those words of strength and chasteness and beauty in which he was wont to clothe his no less strong and chaste and beautiful thoughts. Those lips will never again convey comfort to the sorrowful, and strength to the dying. We bow to the will of Providence. Upon Him whose throne is built on righteousness, we rest. " Clouds and darkness are round about Him: righteousness and judgment are the habitation of His Throne." We mark it as an evidence of Divine love that our revered friend was so long spared to us, to counsel us by his wisdom, to encourage us by his example, to cheer us by his friendship. And that he has died full of days and full of honour, surrounded by affectionate children, and faithful relatives and friends who have watched and cared for him, with, I may say, unexampled devotion, we accept also as a mark of the Divine favour. But that in the midst of very great sufferings he should have retained his faith and courage, that in the certain prospect of dissolution he should have remained calm and unshaken, that death should have become to him a welcome visitant, that unflinchingly and without even the shadow of fear he should have cried out for release—this is an evidence of Divine mercy, the strength and depth of which I cannot find words to express.

During a ministry of three-and-thirty years, I have witnessed many a death-bed : I never witnessed one in which Christian faith seemed so strong and abiding, and, at the same time, so characteristic. Often, very often, did our friend cry out in his petitions, " Come, Lord Jesus, come quickly! Into Thy hands I commend my spirit, Thou hast redeemed me, Lord God of truth. " Then he would dwell upon the faith of the old patriarchs and try to make it his own; and his it truly was—simple, strong, sustaining. " The Lord Jehovah is my strength and my song, He also is become my salvation. " But the words on which he seemed most to rest were those of the Psalmist already quoted, " into Thy hands I commend my spirit, Thou *hast* redeemed me. " Of our version of the psalms, specially dear to him were the 23rd, 46th and 116th. His favourite death-bed hymn was the 5th, for the reading of which he often called, and which I myself had the privilege of reading to him a few hours before his death.

> " The hour of my departure's come,
> " I hear the voice that calls me home,
> " At last, O Lord, let troubles cease
> " And let Thy servant die in peace."

If you ask me in what faith he died, I could not give you a truer formula than the 3rd verse of this hymn :

> " Not in mine innocence I trust
> " I bow before Thee in the dust,
> " And through my Saviour's blood alone
> " I look for mercy at Thy Throne."

I could tell you a great deal more of what our friend thought and said and believed, but it is not needful.

Why do I say aught at all? Because I feel it right that you should know how your minister died. Right that you should be told that the truths which he so often spoke to you from the pulpit, and at the sick-bed, sufficed to sustain *him* in the trying hour; gave him victory over doubt, over fear, over death itself.

And now we bear away to its last resting place this noble and once majestic form ! Corruptible, it shall put on incorruption ; mortal, it shall put on immortality ; sown in weakness, it shall be raised in power ; sown in corruption it shall be raised in incorruption ; sown a natural body, it shall be raised a spiritual body ; even in that day when the trumpet of the Archangel shall sound, and shall summon from their graves the righteous dead. Then shall be brought to pass the saying that is written " Death is swallowed up in victory ! "

Prayer was then offered for the bereaved family, for the congregation, for the ministry and eldership, and for the whole Catholic Church, after which the congregation joined in singing the 3rd and 5th verses of the fifth Hymn, and received the Apostolic Benediction.

A large number of the members of St. Andrew's Church availed themselves of the opportunity afforded them to take a last look at the placid features of their late minister, while the doleful, deep-sounding notes of the "Dead March in Saul" were pealed forth from the great organ.

A greater mark of funeral respect has seldom been paid to a citizen of Montreal. Taken as a whole it was a grand spectacle, and the ceremony was of a most impressive character. On leaving the church the procession reformed and proceeded to Mount Royal Cemetery, in one of the vaults of which was deposited all that is mortal of one concerning whom it may be said, as of the great Scottish Reformer: "HERE LIES ONE WHO NEVER FEARED THE FACE OF MAN."

At a meeting of St. Andrew's congregation, held on the 24th February, 1870, the following minute in reference to their late minister, was unanimously adopted:

"The congregation of St. Andrew's Church think it becoming in them to express the very high estimation in which they held their late much lamented pastor, the Rev. Alexander Mathieson, D.D., and to recognize his great services to the Church, and to the cause of religion in Canada, as well as to the congregation in particular; also, to bear testimony to his pre-eminent virtues, dignity of character, large hearted benevolence, geniality of disposition, true nobility of nature, joined with simple piety and a pure life, which so endeared him to all, and, more especially, to the congregation over which he so long presided, and to whom he dispensed the Bread of Life."

A minute of similar import to the foregoing, was also adopted by the Kirk Session of St. Andrew's Church, at their first meeting, after the death of " their late Moderator, Pastor, and Friend."

———

The entire press of Canada joined in the general tribute of respect that was paid to the memory of Dr. Mathieson, on the announcement of his decease, thus affording a gratifying and convincing proof that his many noble qualities of head and heart were duly appreciated by his fellow subjects of all creeds and denominations, of all nationalities and shades of politics. We have only room for the concluding passage of an article occuppying two columns of the Montreal *Herald*, in which particular allusion is made to his connection with the St. Andrew's Society of Montreal. "Of Dr. Mathieson it may be said that he was a universal favourite with all he came in contact, being much beloved by his flock, who looked to him as their Father. To all he was affable and courteous, the poor being special objects of his care; and, as he said on his retirement from office in the St. Andrew's Society, in the fall of 1869, his aim was not to foster pauperism, but to give the applicants for aid, first, work, and then assistance. His connection with the St. Andrew's Society was from the date of its foundation in 1835, when he was elected its first chaplain. On the 30th November, 1836, he preached the first annual sermon,

A MONUMENT TO HIS MEMORY.

and, in 1868, he preached his last sermon in connection with it, from the words, " walk about Zion," &c. His discourses were peculiarly appropriate to the occasions on which they were delivered, and so touching were some of his allusions to the " land of the mountain and the flood," and her glorious Institutions, that his hearers were visibly affected. The Reverend Doctor was twenty-five times elected chaplain of this Benevolent Society, and was always regular in attendance at the committee meetings, and ever ready to assist them in their labours of love.

Photography has preserved for us some admirable and life-like portraits of the late venerable minister of St. Andrew's Church. But it is worthy of consideration whether or not a substantial and enduring monument should be erected to the memory of so worthy a citizen of Montreal as Dr. Mathieson was. Along-side of the Anglican Cathedral, an elaborate and costly monument is in course of construction to commemorate the services to his Church, during eighteen years, of the late excellent Bishop of Montreal. If what we have said, and what others have said, who were less likely than we to be biassed in their estimate of Dr. Mathieson's character and services be true, the Presbyterians of Montreal would do honour to themselves in placing along-side of St. Andrew's Church, a statue of its late minister, who was for a much longer period the recognized head and representative of Presbyterianism in the city. Whatever expense might be incurred in carrying out such a proposal would be cheerfully shared by all the congregations of the Church.

Extract from a sermon preached in St. Andrew's Church, Toronto, by the Rev. Dr. Barclay, on Psalm cvii., 7, "He led them forth by the right way that they might go to a city of habitation."

It is unspeakably precious and consoling, amid earthly separations, to think that the completed journey of a true Christian life is but the arrival at the end of "the right way" which leads to "the city of habitation." There are households amongst us where such testimony has but recently been borne to the value of religion as a guide through that way, to the rest on high. Valuable are the lessons which thus come—whether from high or from humble homes—loud the calls thus uttered, strong the inducements thus presented to us all, to be "followers of those who are now inheriting the promises."

In thus reviewing the text, in the admonitions it lifts, my thoughts turn with saddened interest to an old and much-valued friend, recently departed, whose prominent position in the Church, during a lengthened ministerial life, entitles him to public notice from any of her pulpits; and over whose unexpected decease I desire here to give expression to my own heartfelt sympathies, in the regret I feel at the separation from us of one so worthy of all honour, whose face we shall not again behold in this land of living men. I refer to the late Rev. Dr. Mathieson of Montreal, whose name has been so long and intimately associated with the history of the Church of Scotland in this land, and whose many noble qualities secured for him the respect and regard of a large circle of friends, who highly appreciated his worth, and will long cherish his memory.

Of a commanding presence and dignified deportment, unselfish, and free from all that savoured of a mean or sordid nature—possessing warm sympathies, and of a generous disposition, with great kindness of heart—he was peculiarly fitted to occupy a position of prominence among his fellow-men, whilst he enjoyed in large measure, the esteem of those who were privileged to associate with him.

Coming to this country previous to the organization of the Synod he has thus been connected with our Church, in active ministerial service, for nearly half a century. Occupying as he did a leading place in our Communion, as the minister of one of the most important of our congregations—his first and only ministerial charge; fitted by his talents, by his weight of character, and by his indomitable energy and steadfastness of purpose, to take a leading part in the Church's counsels and in conducting its public affairs; warmly attached to the Church of Scotland and desirous of imitating, or emulating, all that was praiseworthy in the venerable Parent, by a close adherence to its model in organizing and consolidating our Church in this land, his influence was felt in the leading emergencies in its history. He has left his impress on many of its acts, and had a large share in the shaping of its policy and in the direction of its affairs; whilst in all that concerned the welfare of the Church he took the deepest interest, and devoted thereto no small portion of his time and energy.

To the consideration of all questions affecting the position and public interests of the Church he brought a sound judgment and thoroughly honest convictions, which he never abandoned for the suggestions, however plausible, of a doubtful expediency; whilst he

X

uniformly exhibited a straightforwardness of purpose in the firm assertion of what he believed to be right, and to which he clung with a resoluteness not easily if ever shaken. He might be mistaken in some of his plans, but he was never other than sincere in upholding them. Stable in his friendships, of a genial temperament, and ever ready by his counsel and his means to help all who sought his aid, he might sometimes be deceived by those who abused his confidence, yet in high principle and generous sentiment he showed the true nobility of his nature, the disinterestedness of his friendship, and the reality of his sterling worth.

A perspicuous and graceful writer, with a naturally vigorous intellect and of a philosophic turn; having a mind well stored with the acquirements of early study, and thoroughly embued with the importance and magnitude of the great themes to which the efforts of the pulpit are devoted; and with a heart quietly and unostentatiously responding to their influence, he took high rank as an intelligent and instructive expounder of God's Word, to which honourable and responsible work so many years of his life have been devoted.

Though not usually demonstrative in his piety he was nevertheless true to his religious convictions, and clear in his apprehensions of divine truth; and his latter end, as testified to by those who were privileged to witness the gradually closing scene of his long and honoured life, was distinguished by a peculiar firmness of faith, and trustful dependence on the Saviour, to whom he looked with unshaken confidence in the prospect of dissolution.

I have been expounding to you this day some of the features of a true christian as set forth in the text, and the character of " the way" by which he walks in the pilgrimage of life, with as much clearness as my own apprehension of them enabled me, and with such fulness as the present opportunity has afforded; but I point you also to the record of the like truth as written in the history of a departed believer, whose aim was to walk in that way, humbly and unostentatiously serving the Lord. He had passed the three score years and ten usually allotted to man, and the way for him was therefore not a "*short*" one. Whether, and to what extent, amid the dark shadows of bereavements which passed over his dwelling, and other trials that skirt the path of life, it may have been to him, not the "easy way," nor the way that was free from perplexities, we cannot fully tell. But the way, we trust, it has been for him to the "city of habitation." "Behold the upright, for the latter end of that man is peace."

From many quarters, and in varied forms, admonitions are perpetually coming to persuade us of the benefits of walking in "the right way" as strangers and pilgrims on the earth—thus consecrating to God's service the talents, whether the two, or the ten, He has given us to "occupy," we may make the journey of life a pilgrimage to the better land. Give heed then, to the lessons of true wisdom; walk in her ways as defined by Christ Himself, and exemplified in His own holy life; cherish that true hope which rests on this Rock of Ages, as set forth in the great charter of our faith, and commended to us by the life and death of the good and true of our fellow-men; so that over your completed life there may at length fall to be written in the language of truth an epitaph, embodying the sentiment of the text: "He was led forth by the right way that he might go to a city of habitation."

Funeral Sermon.

In accordance with ecclesiastical custom the members of the Presbytery of Montreal, who attended Dr. Mathieson's funeral met in the vestry of St. Paul's Church, immediately after the interment. The Rev. Donald Ross,, B.D., acting as Moderator: when the Rev. John Jenkins, D.D., was appointed to preach to the congregation of St. Andrew's, on the following Sabbath, and also to act as moderator of the Kirk Session, until the next meeting of the Presbytery.

The funeral sermon that now follows, was accordingly preached by Dr. Jenkins, on the 20th of February, 1870, in the Hall of the Normal School, in Belmont street, where the congregation of St. Andrew's have worshipped since the destruction of their Church by fire.

FUNERAL SERMON.

BEHOLD, I SHEW YOU A MYSTERY: WE SHALL NOT ALL SLEEP, BUT WE SHALL ALL BE CHANGED, IN A MOMENT, IN THE TWINKLING OF AN EYE, AT THE LAST TRUMP; FOR THE TRUMPET SHALL SOUND, AND THE DEAD SHALL BE RAISED INCORRUPTIBLE, AND WE SHALL BE CHANGED, &c.—*I Corinthians* xv, 51.

PLINY, an accomplished writer and philosopher of ancient times, maintained the opinion that two things are impossible to the Creator: One, The bestowment upon mortals of endless life, the other, The resurrection of the dead. He speaks, elsewhere, of the resuscitation of the dead as "a childish, doting story." Æschylus, a disciple of the Pythagorean school, was also of opinion that it is beyond the power of Deity to raise from death a human body. This was the universal doctrine of ancient speculation.

We read, in the Acts of the Apostles, that, in Athens, certain philosophers of the Epicureans and of the Stoics encountered Paul, crying out, "What will this babbler say?" and, "He seemeth to be a setter forth of strange gods?" Why this reproach? The historian supplies the reason: "Because he preached unto them Jesus and the resurrection." From these sources, and from others which might be readily named, we learn that the world by wisdom kn w not the doctrine which is so authoritatively announced and so strikingly illustrated in this remarkable chapter.

This doctrine of the resurrection of the dead is a doctrine of pure revelation. The ancients needed the first sentence of the Bible to prepare them for their researches into the laws of nature. Their ignorance of the fact that " in the beginning GOD created the heavens and the earth," led to their acceptance of the theory of the eternity of matter. So, they who thought the creation of something out of nothing impossible, were ill-prepared to admit the resurrection of corrupted, dissolved and dissipated bodies. Even the doctrine of the immortality of the soul was held with doubt; and was taught, not so much because it was believed, as that it was deemed a powerful check upon the morals of the masses. Numerous proofs of this might be supplied from the Greek and Latin classics. There were vague imaginings of immortality as the end of this mutable and sorrowful life; but they never assumed a palpable conception. How uncertain were the views of the old philosophers on the subject of a future state may be seen from the avidity with which they embraced the doctrine of the transmigration of souls, which Pythagoras first learned from the Hindoos, and then disseminated throughout Greece.

I mention these facts that you may be assisted to appreciate the value of the Bible; especially of that portion of the Sacred Writings which constitutes the basis of Christian teaching — to appreciate the elevation to which you are raised by your connection with Christianity. I would you should feel how superior in true sublimity and certainty of teaching is the Gospel system to every other. I confidently challenge a comparison of the clearest deliverances of antiquity on this and kindred subjects, with the clear, consecutive, profound, eloquent and conclusive reasoning which Paul presents to us in this chapter. There is a power in the Apostle's language, a felicity of illustration, a transparency of instruction, which seem to cast every other author into the shade. It is the light of day quenching the glimmering of tiny stars! It is the glory of the sun dissipating the clouds of uncertainty, dispelling the darkness of error!

The obscurity which enveloped the teaching of the Old Testament on the subject of immortality and the resurrection was partially relieved when Jesus cried out before the sepulchre of Lazarus, "I am the resurrection and the life. He that believeth in Me, though he were dead yet shall he live, and whosoever liveth and believeth in Me shall never die." Still further was this obscurity dispelled when the Redeemer was Himself raised from the dead by the glory of the Father.

In this chapter another, may I not say the last, step is taken. Every difficulty is cleared away; every doubt dissipated; the whole subject stated with unquestionable authority. Our Apostle has left nothing to be added. It is as though he had exhausted the subject; as though, in truth, he had stretched forth his hand and snatched away every remnant of the veil which before intercepted man's view into the future. One truth he enunciates which was never before disclosed—a truth which, up to the moment when his pen inscribed our text, was involved in mystery; a truth, ignorance of which constituted an obstinate difficulty in the investigation of the whole subject. Granted that the bodies of the dead are to be raised; granted that the scattered dust of mortals shall be collected and re-constructed into glorious bodies; what is to become of the millions that shall be alive at the appearing of Christ? Shall their bodies remain as they are?—or shall they die and their remains be scattered over the earth for a brief time so that they may share resurrection blessings? Moses throws no light upon the subject; the prophets do not unveil the mystery; even Christ is silent; and we have no knowledge till Paul steps forth and says: " Behold, I show you a mystery : we shall not all sleep but we shall all be changed, in a moment, in the twinkling of an eye, at the last trump."

I have thought that nothing could be more instructive or comforting to you in the solemn circumstances in which we meet than a consideration of this great subject. You will not expect me, after what was said on occasion of the burial of your late revered pastor, to speak to you again of his qualities as a minister, as a Christian and as a man. You have learned what they were by long observation, and by the largest experience. Let me rather raise your thoughts this morning, the thoughts especially of you who have lately been bereaved, to that " life and immortality " which the Gospel brings to light, and the hope of which is alone our support in the bereavements of time;—that immortal life of believers which is "hid with Christ in God." In the light of revelation we regard our venerable and venerated friend not as dead, but as asleep; resting in Christ until he shall awake in the morning of the resurrection. Paganism looks into human graves despondingly, and takes a last, an eternal farewell of those who die. Christianity commits the bodies of believers to the grave with confidence and hope akin to those with which the husbandman casts seed into the ground. Your late minister sleepeth! But methinks I hear the voice of Jesus whispering in our ear the hope-giving words, "Your pastor, brother, friend shall rise again!" The trumpet shall sound, and then the Saviour will come to awake him out of sleep!

The text furnishes a description of what shall take place at the sounding of the last trump, and of the triumphant scenes which shall follow.

"*The trumpet shall sound.*" Elsewhere it is called "the trump of God;" again, "the last trump." The reference is to the coming of the Lord, when He shall descend from heaven with the voice of the Archangel, and when "the dead in Christ shall rise first."

There was the sound of a trumpet on Sinai at the giving of the law; it shook the mountain to its base, and the people did exceedingly fear and quake. The voice of the last trump shall shake the world. We infer that there will be but one blast, for it shall be accomplished "in a moment, in the twinkling of an eye;" be this as it may, it shall be so deep, so loud, so thrilling, that there shall be no part of this vast earth in which it shall not be heard, no cavern of the dead which its sound shall not enter, no sea nor ocean the depths of which shall not be penetrated by its voice: "The trumpet shall sound."

"*And the dead shall be raised incorruptible.*" This, we have said, is a doctrine of pure revelation. The attempt has been made to prove the future resurrection of the dead on simply natural principles. It has been wholly unsuccessful. Contrariwise, an effort has been made, on the same principles, to demonstrate its impossibility. I shall not enumerate the objections which have been raised against the doctrine of the resurrection. I resolve them by a reference to the Almighty, with whom all things are possible; and by a reference also to the Word of God, from which there is no appeal.

St. Paul, in the chapter before us, speaks of the resurrection of the *righteous* dead. Respecting the *wicked* it is only needful for me to say here, that they too shall rise; but it shall be " to shame and everlasting contempt."

The *righteous* dead shall be raised incorruptible. It has been attempted to fritter away this teaching of our apostle by the theory that the future bodies of the saints shall not be identical with those which they now have. You see at once, that to accept such a theory would be, virtually, to abandon the doctrine of the resurrection altogether. If the same body be not meant, then were it a contradiction in terms to call it a resurrection. That it will be greatly changed we learn from both the statements and the illustrations contained in this chapter. No longer natural, it shall be a spiritual body; no longer earthly, it shall be a heavenly body. But that its identity will be maintained—maintained in some sufficient sense, is clearly given to us as the opinion of the Apostles, The objection to the statement of the Apostle in the text, has been urged on the ground of the magnitude of the miracle which a general resurrection involves. It is deemed too stupendous for credibility. In the estimation of these objectors it cannot be that the scattered dust of the innumerable dead shall be collected and re-formed; but it may be that other bodies will be constructed from other dust. The Creator could, *did*, construct a body for man, yea, an immortal body, from the dust of the earth, impressing it with grace and beauty and even majesty; but now that this body has returned " to the dust as it was," He cannot re-construct it into a body like unto Christ's glorious body! It is too much to suppose that the Divine Being could watch over this dust for five or seven thousand years, and at the end of this period re-invest it with life and beauty! Could he care for this dust and protect it for a day? why not for a thousand years? seeing that " one day is with the Lord as a thousand years, and a thousand years as one day." Narrow, imperfect must be the views of these sceptical Christians concerning the perfections of God! What is all time to Him who inhabiteth eternity? What the preservation of the dust of millions to Him who is almighty and omnipresent? What the care of dead bodies, as they lie entombed in the earth, to Him who cares for fifteen hundred millions of living bodies every moment of every year? This *corruptible* shall put on incorruption; this *mortal* shall put on immortality. The *dead* shall hear the voice of the Son of God; and they that hear shall live." " All that are in the *graves* shall hear the voice of the Son of Man. " Take these texts; accept them in their simple meaning; give them a place in your intellects and your hearts. When you lay the remains of the departed in the grave draw comfort from the promise that from this very sepulchre the stone shall be removed, that this very grave shall be re-opened, that this very body shall be re-animated with life, that these ears shall hear the last trump, these eyes, now dark and sunken, gaze with rapture on the Son of God, the Saviour, these lips, closed and livid, shout the noble pœan, "Thanks be unto God who giveth us the victory through our Lord Jesus Christ." You have laid in yonder cemetery a father, a pastor, a husband, a wife, a child. Sorrow not as those without hope. They only sleep, and are gathering new vigour for the morning of the resurrection and the day of eternity.

Emblems of the resurrection meet you on every hand. Nature is full of them. See that worm, it lives, it crawls, it spins its silk, it seems to die; the chrysalis lies in torpor; by-and-bye it bursts its shell, it expands its wings, and flies away with new life, invested with a grace, a loveliness, a beauty which it did not before possess. This is a resurrection. Will you say that it is not the same worm which crawled at your feet, that now attracts you by its grace and loveliness? What is morning but the resurrection of day from the death of night? The day dies, and is buried in silence and in darkness; it bursts the tomb of night, and rises in glory. Here, says Tertullian, you have before your eyes a daily emblem of the doctrine, a diurnal resurrection. What is winter but death? The sap, the life of vegetation, descends into the roots and is buried in the ground; the earth is covered with snow or crusted with frost, and becomes one vast sepulchre; but when spring appears, the plants and flowers come out of their graves and rise in beauteous life. Every seed as it falls from the tree is an emblem at once of death and of the resurrection. It falls into the earth and rots; but it contains the germ of life, and in a little while sprouts and shoots and lives again in grace and vigour.

You reply, that these facts in nature afford no proof of the resurrection of the body. I know it. But they surely suggest both the possibility and even probability of such a transformation. At least there is no absurdity involved in this article of the Christian creed, " I believe in the resurrection of the dead," natural science being itself judge. There is point in the reproof and rejoinder of Paul, " thou fool, that which thou sowest is not quickened, except it die."

" *This corruptible must put on incorruption, and this mortal must put on immortality.*" It *must*, that it may become a fit casket for the glorified spirit; for how can that which is carnal, mortal and corruptible, enjoy that which is spiritual, immortal, and imperishable? Here you have the reason for the change which shall be wrought in the bodies of those believers who shall be alive at the coming of the Lord. Although they shall not die, yet shall they undergo a transformation equivalent to that which the raised dead shall have undergone; their bodies shall be made incorruptible, immortal, like unto Christ's glorious body. Have we not here an incidental proof of the identity of the resurrection of the body? It will not be denied that, in the case of those who remain unto the coming of Christ, the same body shall be renewed and glorified. But you at once give these a superiority for which you have no scriptural warrant, if you deny the *general* identity of the raised and transformed body. " The dead shall be raised incorruptible and we shall be changed." " This," says Paul in one of his Thessalonian Epistles, " this we say unto you by the word of the Lord, that we which remain unto the coming of the Lord shall not go before them that are asleep, for the Lord Himself shall descend from heaven with a shout, with the voice of the Archangel, and the trump of God, and the dead in Christ shall rise first. Then we which are alive and remain shall be caught up together with them in the clouds, to meet the Lord in the air: and so shall we ever be with the Lord. Wherefore comfort one another with these words."

Contemplate the triumphant scenes which shall follow the resurrection and transformation of the bodies of the saints.

"*Then shall be brought to pass the saying that is written, Death is swallowed up in victory.*" This is a quotation from one of Isaiah's prophecies concerning Christ. You find it in the twenty-fifth chapter: " He will swallow up death in victory!" The expression suggests conflict. Strong and protracted has been the conflict between death and the saints of the Most High! It still goes on. But now the conflict shall be ended; and the victory shall be Christ's and His people's. The victory shall be yours, my brethren, as in anticipation it was that of your late Minister, when with joy and trust he cried out, as life was ebbing, "Into Thy Hands I commend my spirit. Thou hast redeemed me, Lord God of truth."

Look at the pledges of your future conquest over death: Go to Zarephath, into the widow's house, and see death conquered by the effectual fervent prayer of righteous Elijah! Go to the grave of Elisha, and behold germs of life in the very bones of the prophet! Go to Ezekiel's valley of vision, and see there death dissipated by the breath of the Spirit! You say it is only a parable. Yet it proves that the reality is practicable. Go to Nain, and see in the restoration of the widow's son that death is held in subjection to the will of Jesus! Go to the tomb of Lazarus, and behold in his liberation from death's prison-house the power over death of the voice of the Son of God. Go! Search the tomb of Christ, and see in that vacated sepulchre, a pledge that He will at length " swallow up death in victory," and that mortality shall be swallowed up of life." Death shall be swallowed up! Complete shall be the conquest. Death shall be swallowed up! never again to appear; never more to exert his power or use his sting. Death shall be swallowed up! for Christ shall put all enemies under His feet; "the last enemy that shall be destroyed is death." "Death and Hades shall be cast into the lake of fire." There shall be no more sin and no more curse, and so, "there shall be no more death."

"*Death is swallowed up in victory.*" With what joy shall the saints survey this conquest over their last surviving foe! Looking back over this world's scenes, when death wrung out tears and groans, and provoked many a conflict, when widows shrieked and orphans wept, and parents mourned over the graves of the departed;—looking back, I say, upon these scenes, and comparing them with what shall then be,

"Wonder and joy shall fill their heart,
And love command their tongue."

Can you be surprised at the exultation with which it is here foretold the saints shall be inspired? Can you wonder at the defiance with which it is represented they shall insult their vanquished foe? Judging from his language, the idea suggested to the Apostle's mind was that of the whole multitude of the raised and glorified dead—an immense assemblage—looking down with defiance upon the monster-foe, stingless and disarmed, giving utterance to a song of universal triumph. It is a lofty conception! The whole body of the redeemed constituting one vast choir: Some of them singing "O death, where is thy sting?" Others of them responding, "O grave, where is thy victory?" Some, again, chaunting, "The sting of death is sin!" Others, taking up the chaunt and replying, "The strength of sin is the law!" And then, the whole body breaking forth in one grand ecstatic chorus, "Thanks be unto God which giveth us the victory through our Lord Jesus Christ." O that we might be present on that great occasion! O that we might listen to the triumphant song! O that we might help to chaunt its wondrous melodies!

"*Through Jesus Christ our Lord!*" This is the climax of the wondrous chorus. It is Christ who hath abolished death. He hath banished him from his own domain—the Church of the redeemed. His blood is the price paid down as a ransom for the deliverance from death of both the bodies and the souls of His chosen ones. And this blood, and the atonement which it made, shall be the chief theme in all the praises of the glorified in heaven: "Thou wast slain and hast redeemed us unto God by Thy blood, out of every nation and kindred and people and tongue." "Thanks be to God, which giveth us the victory through our Lord Jesus Christ."

But for Christ, death would have remained victor, and our bodies would have been for ever held in the bondage of the grave. But for Christ, Paganism would have been right; silence and gloom, unbroken and impenetrable, would have brooded over every human grave. But for Christ, the glories of the resurrection morn would never dawn upon the world; the grave would remain for ever closed; the caverns of the sea would for ever hold fast their dead. But for Christ, the saints would never walk forth from their graves in the robes of immortality, and the universe would never witness the glorious spectacle of a redeemed world shouting victory over death.

How much owe we to Christ! Have we peace? He is its author. Are we holy? His blood has cleansed us. Have we hope? Christ is in us the hope of glory. Are we sustained in our bereavements? It is because our friends whom we have buried out of our sight "sleep in Jesus."

I come to you to-day with a solemn message. I am commissioned by the Presbytery to proclaim this Charge vacant. Already are you called to take steps to fill the place of him who for more than three and forty years presided over your interests as a congregation, and ministered to you the Word of Life. There will be other ministers of St. Andrew's Church;—there will never be buried a minister of this congregation, who will have more earnestly thought and worked for his people than he whose funeral we attended on Thursday. To the very last his heart was here, going out in affection for his people, anxiously desiring the future prosperity of the church for whose interests he so long laboured and so successfully. There were in him resources of power, intellectual and moral, not often found in the ministry; or this church would not be what it is, to day, in numbers, in liberality, in influence, in true power. It is not pretended that he was always right! Who is always right? But it is claimed that he was always conscientious and that he ever sought, so far as he was able to apprehend, the best interests of St. Andrew's Church. That he was a grateful minister, feeling to an almost distressing keenness the kindnesses which he occasionally received from his flock, none can doubt. The sympathy extended to him in the overwhelming sorrow which befel him eighteen months ago was so deeply felt as to be utterly inexpressible; and the graceful token of respect for him, and for her whom he mourned, which some of you evinced in the erection of that beautiful memorial destroyed by the calamity of the 24th of October, lodged itself in his heart with undying gratitude. I shall read to you the sentences which he penned in regard to this ubject, and which he clearly purposed sending to those who had thus contributed to his sad joy. These, his words, shall be my last words to you to-day. They are found in an unfinished note, penned, evidently, under deep emotion—an emotion so deep as that he was unable to finish it. It would seem, indeed, to have been written in a reverie of overwhelming grief mixed with gratitude:

Montreal, 4th Nov., 1867.

My D——: Language is inadequate to express my gratitude for your kindness in raising a memorial window in remembrance of my dear Janet Ewing Mathieson. I can only thank you, which I do from the very bottom of my heart.

The frail memorial, like her lovely life, has passed away; teaching us not to fix our affections on any earthly blessings, but to fix them on the things that are above. May the Divine Spirit affix on our hearts the truth so impressively taught.

Your sympathetic memorial took me somewhat by surprise. My emotions were too deep. I could not look on it without unmanly weakness. From the glance I gave to it, it appeared to me very beautiful. When they somewhat subside, I hope to contemplate it with composure.

* * * *

PART II.

.

THREE DISCOURSES

Preached by Dr. Mathieson,

ON

Different Occasions.

THE writers of discourses for the pulpit are, of all men, the most subject to interruptions in their literary labours, and it cannot be expected that they will be always equally successful in style and matter. In proportion to the number of sermons from which a selection is required to be made is the difficulty of fixing upon such as may be esteemed the best, or the most suitable for publication. In the present instance, the amount of time and labour that would be required in making a judicious choice are such as quite preclude the attempt. It is therefore proper to state that the following sermons are offered to the public chiefly on account of the historical interest which is supposed to attach to them, rather than from their intrinsic literary merits—though, at the same time, they afford evidence of careful preparation and of high mental culture.

The first sermon preached by Dr. Mathieson in Montreal, the last sermon preached by him before the Synod, and, the last, to the Congregation of St. Andrew's, will, it is confidently hoped, be accepted as a pleasing souvenir of their author, and a suitable accompaniment to these memoirs.

SERMON I.*

Brethren, pray for us, that the Word of the Lord may have free course and be glorified.—II *Thessalonians* iii. 1.

My Christian Brethren and Friends—Having, with the customary solemnities, been invested with the pastoral charge of this congregation, I this day enter on the public performance of the very important duties of that office—duties deriving their importance at once from the authoritative sanction of Almighty God, whose ambassador to you, with the overtures of peace and reconciliation, I profess to be, and also, from the intimate connexion which the discharge of these duties has with the happiness or misery of your undying souls; for the faithful minister of His Word is always unto God a sweet savour of Christ in them that are saved and in them that perish; to the one he is the savour of death unto death, and to the other the savour of life unto life.

(*) This was the first sermon preached by Dr. Mathieson in St. Andrew's Church, Montreal—on the last Sabbath of 1826. It was delivered by him again on the last Sabbath of 1869, a very short time before the close of his ministerial labours.

The arduous and difficult nature of the duties of the ministerial office bears a relative proportion to their supreme importance. This, in part, arises from the nature of the office itself, the great end and aim of which is the recovery of fallen and degraded men to their original purity and happiness; the enlightening of their understandings who are spiritually blind; the communication of truth to the minds of those who are dead in trespasses and sins; the production of principles which will bring forth fruit unto everlasting life in the souls of them who are at utter enmity with God, and habitually addicted to all that is impure and unholy.

In attempting to realize these great ends of the Christian ministry, it is obvious, from the nature of the employment, that difficulties and discouragements of no ordinary magnitude stand in the way. There is a levity and carelessness of disposition, and an indifference to whatsoever is of a spiritual nature, that are characteristics of human apostacy, which too often oppose themselves, at the very threshold, to the reception of the Gospel. Should the faithful minister of Christ succeed in breaking down this formidable barrier, and awakening in the minds of His people a just sense of their danger, still he will find that the unrenewed principles of humanity will disqualify him from willingly accepting the plan which God, in His wisdom, devised, and by His Almighty power wrought out for the salvation of sinners, and which in the Gospel of His Son is so clearly revealed. His pride refuses to be humbled, and will not tolerate the communication of truths which fasten the charge of guilt and depravity on the conscience. His selfishness and vanity will but little dispose him to rely with humble confidence for salvation on *His* merits alone whom God hath set forth to be the only propitiation for sin, and few indeed will be found who sit so loose to the world and its pleasures as to make those self-sacrifices which the Gospel requires, and unreluctantly forego the gratifications of sense for enjoyments that are pure and spiritual, and which can only be discerned by the eye of an enlightened and discriminating faith.

Thus opposed to the prejudices and passions of men, the truths of the Gospel will be regarded with aversion, or rejected with disdain by many, while its ministers, instead of being welcomed with joy, as the harbingers of happiness and peace, will be traduced as messengers of evil tidings, and propagators of a dark and gloomy superstition, adapted only to abridge the number of our social enjoyments and give a forbidding aspect to all the pleasures of life. And should the minister of Christ be the honoured instrument of awakening the minds of those committed to his charge to a just sense of the danger of their condition, and instructing them in the knowledge of those truths that are intimately connected with their salvation, still he will find that here his labours end not. His strenuous and persevering efforts will still be necessary to convert their speculative knowledge into active principles. This, unquestionably, is the work of a higher agent than man, a work which only Omnipotence can effect, still, as God chooses to work by means, and as He hath set apart an order of men expressly for the purpose of carrying forward His designs with respect to our fallen race, not to avail ourselves of the means which are of His appointment—means which He hath put within our reach, and promised to bless, would be as derogatory to His honour as it would be altogether to deny our dependence on Him. Regarding the

Christian ministry as an instrument in God's hands for advancing Christ's kingdom in the world, and building up from the ruins of humanity a holy and spiritual temple in which the Most High God will condescend to dwell, unquestionably, it is the most important occupation in which a man can be employed, demanding uncompromising fidelity, and unwearied devotedness, until the image of God, after which man was created, again beautify and bless every individual committed to his charge. O how anxiously must he tend the germ of divine truth implanted in the soul, lest the deceitfulness of sin, and the secret insinuations of the spirits of darkness (for we wrestle not only with flesh and blood, but with principalities and powers, the rulers of the darkness of this world and spiritual wickedness in high places) should wither it in the bud, before the early dawning of conviction grow into that elevated piety, which the darkness of guilt cannot obscure nor the temptations of the world ever shake. How diligently must he watch the progress of the divine life in the soul, lest the cares and vanities of life should stifle it in its origin and tempt to repose the hopes of salvation on the transient feelings of love or devotion—which casual circumstances, or a scrupulous observance of the formalities of religion, awaken—instead of unqualifiedly surrendering every thought and feeling, every word and action to the service of God. How frequently and earnestly must he expostulate with sinners on the folly of their ways, and again and again entreat them, by all that is tender and encouraging in mercy, and by all that is awful in the consideration of death, judgment and eternity, to crucify the world with its lusts, and be reconciled unto God. With what delicate taste and discriminating judgment must he convey his instructions, so as to suit the capacities, the character and circumstances of each individual, teaching the rich and powerful to be humble and charitable, the poor and oppressed to be patient and resigned to the dispensations of Providence; repressing the voice of the murmurer, checking the spirit of the arrogant, consoling the afflicted, and comforting the penitent, without infusing the elements of false peace into his soul; rousing the careless and obdurate, and yet so as not to break the bruised reed, nor inflame the wounds of the contrite spirit; bearing home to theconsciences of all men the convictions of sin, and yet avoiding even the appearance of personality; in a word, approving himself unto God a workman that needeth not to be ashamed, rightly dividing the word of truth.

How carefully, also, must he qualify himself for the performance of his duties, by devoting many an hour to the exhausting exercise of intense thought, and to acquaint himself with the general dictates of inspiration, that he may not speak in God's name what He hath not spoken, but plant " wholly a right seed : " How patiently must he cultivate those dispositions and habits, which will make his personal conduct a practical illustration of the doctrines he teaches. How carefully must he strive to elevate his principles and purify his motives, that he may neither be seduced by the applause of the world, and become vain, ostentatious, or indolent nor be tempted to despond when he finds his affection and love repaid with contempt, and when a seemingly impenetrable ignorance and insensibility resist his efforts to instruct or improve those committed to his care. Amidst the weariness and mental distractions which these labours entail, often will he envy the condition of the sons of bodily toil, who, when the day's hard task is done, can quietly resign themselves to the sweets of oblivious repose, and the protection of that gracious Being who watches over them continually, and loads them with His loving-kindness and tender mercies.

When we contemplate the great purposes to be served by the Christian ministry, and the difficulties and discouragements that stand opposed to its success, well may the servants of Christ tremble, and, in the consciousness of their own weakness, exclaim with the Apostle, " Who is sufficient for these things ! "

But although unnumbered difficulties attend the discharge of the functions of the ministry, yet there are many incidents which banish despondency and throw a bright ray of hope over the darkest hour of trial. Bad as the world is, and unconcerned as men generally are about their eternal welfare, the ambassador for Christ will meet with many whose greatest wish is to obtain that salvation which he is commissioned to proclaim, and whose chief happiness is to listen, in the spirit of meekness and docility, to his instructions; whose strenuous exertions will be employed to promote sincere obedience to the precepts he inculcates, and will manifest their gratitude by cultivating that spirity of charity which is the bond of perfectness, and, which, like precious incense on the altar, will diffuse a hallowed influence around. Such considerations will communicate a joy to his soul, which will more than compensate for many an hour of toil and trouble. At the same time the reflection that his success depends not on his own skill or strength, but upon the power of God and the wisdom of God, will banish all distrust arising from the consciousness of his own weakness. He feels, in every difficulty, strong in the Lord, and that, through Christ strengthening him, he can do all things ; hence, brethren, in the work of the ministry, we ought never to view the difficulties to be surmounted in connection with the weakness of the instrument which God hath chosen to accomplish His purposes, except in so far as such a view is calculated to increase our reverence for the ordinances through which He communicates the influences of His Spirit, and to stir us up to make a proper use of them.

But though it be to God, and to him alone, we must look for success, still, the assistance which He vouchsafes to impart, by no means supersedes the necessity of exerting, to the uttermost, our own powers and faculties, and He only bestows His favours in the way of His own appointment. Now, in His Word, we are repeatedly assured, that the conditions on which He is pleased to grant His aid, are, that we ask for it, and cherish it. " Ask and it shall be given you, seek and ye shall find, knock and it shall be opened unto you." "Whatsoever ye shall ask in my name, that will I do." I know no subject of meditation more appropriate to the circumstances in which we are this day assembled, than the request Paul made to the Thessalonian Church, in the words of our text: " Brethren, pray for us, that the word of the Lord may have free course and be glorified, even as it is with you." When we consider the direct effect which this exalted act of devotion has in procuring for us the blessings which we need, or its indirect influence in producing those affections and feelings which dispose us to receive religious instruction with profit, we will be impressed with the conviction that the request which Paul makes in the text, it is our duty to comply with, no less from motives of personal advantage, than the instincts of humanity: " Brethren, pray for us, that the word of the Lord may have free course and be glorified."

That we may more forcibly apply the text to our own case, let us briefly inquire in what way the word of the Lord had free course and was glorified among the Thessalonians. Nor is this an inquiry of little importance, for, undoubtedly, in whatever respects it had free course and was glorified among them, in the same respects and in the same way, in so far as our respective circumstances coincide, it will have free course and be glorified among us.

We are informed by accurate chronologers that Christianity was planted at Thessalonica by Paul about the 50th year of the Christian era. The success of his ministry appears at first to have been very great, for, in his first Epistle, he says " his coming unto them was not in vain." That the Gospel had come unto them, not in word only, but also in power and in the Holy Ghost, and in much assurance, and he thanked God without ceasing, because that when they had received the Word of God, which they had heard of him, they received it not as the word of man, but, as it is in truth, the Word of God. He also tells them that he remembers their work of faith and labour of love; that it was known at Macedonia and Achaia, that they had become followers of the Lord; that they had turned from idols to serve the living God, and to wait for His Son from heaven; that their faith grew exceedingly; that the charity of every one of them all towards each other abounded; that they had faith and patience in all the persecutions they endured; that, as touching brotherly love, there was no need that he should write unto them, as they were taught of God to love one another; that they did so and edified and comforted one another. From these passages you will perceive, how the Word of the Lord had free course and was glorified among the Thessalonians, and also what things ought to be the subjects of your frequent and earnest prayers at the throne of grace. The Christians at Thessalonica glorified the Word of the Lord by the readiness, humility, and joy with which they had received it. They cavilled not at its doctrines, they rejected not its precepts, but gave a willing assent to all its demands. The blessed fruits it produced in them were conversion from the darkness of heathen ignorance and idolatry to the light of the gospel and the service of the living God, to the exercise of patience in all their trials, to the exceeding increase of an enlightened faith, and a widely extended charity. Such are the gifts and graces essential to the character of every Christian. Pray then, brethren, to the Giver of every good and perfect gift that He would pour out in rich effusion, upon all the ministers of His Word, the enlightening, strengthening, sanctifying influences of His Holy Spirit, that they may discern what is the good and perfect and acceptable will of God; that they may search for and find in the pages of inspiration the law of their own lives; and, by a faithful discharge of their duties, recommend the same unerring guide to their several congregations. Pray ye, that the God and Father of "Our Lord Jesus Christ" would give, to every individual they are commissioned to instruct, the Spirit of wisdom and revelation in the knowledge of Him; the eyes of their understanding being enlightened that they may know what is the hope of His calling, and what the riches of the glory of His inheritance in the saints, and what the exceeding greatness of His power in them who believe, so that they may embrace with gratitude the offered salvation, and welcome with joy the glad tidings which angels announced to the shepherds, while their anthems of glory to God in the highest awoke the still slumbers of the night, and their hymns of praise to God, and good-will to men, in sweetest melody, floated on the midnight breezes o'er the plains of Bethlehem. Pray ye, that the Gospel may come unto them, not in word only, but also in power, and in the Holy Ghost, and in much assurance, to extirpate every prejudice from the mind, to subdue every evil propensity, to withdraw their hearts from the world's idolatry, and give the whole homage of their affections unto Him whose inalienable prerogative is the absolute sovereignty of the heart. Pray ye, that they may be endued with the faith that overcometh the world, that charity, the bond of perfectness, may be richly diffused over all the dwellings of men; giving unto all a common object of pursuit, and a reciprocal concern for each other's welfare which will unite them in indestructible harmony. This is the true spirit of the gospel of Christ. In proportion as it prevails the tumult and strife that arise from a collision of conflicting interests are hushed, and wrath and animosity disappear.

It is consistent with the loftiest conceptions we form of an infinitely powerful and benevolent God that He grant an answer in peace to the prayers of unfeigned faith and humility. Explicit declarations, that, " the effectual fervent prayer of a righteous man availeth much;" that, " him that calleth upon God in sincerity and truth He will hear and answer," are scattered over every page of the sacred volume, and are confirmed by the experience of good men in all ages. You have read that when the rebellious Israelites complained, and the anger of the Lord was kindled against them, and His fire consumed them, Moses prayed and the fire was quenched. You have read that the prayers of Joshua arrested the sun in his course until the enemies of the Lord had been destroyed; that the prayers of Elias reanimated the dead, sealed the windows of heaven, so that "it rained not on the earth by the space of three years and six months;" that at his intercession it was re-opened, the rain fell, and the earth brought forth her fruits. You have read that the prayers of Hezekiah brought an angel from heaven to cut off the beleaguering hosts of the Assyrians; that Samuel and John were given in answer to their mother's supplications, and that the venerable Simeon ultimately obtained what had long been the object of his holy desires, and the theme of his constant prayers. But why need I multiply examples of a fact which, I am persuaded, you all acknowledge; many of you, I sincerely hope, from your personal experience. Surely, if the prayers of holy men in times past have been effectual in working miracles, we may reasonably expect that a gracious answer will be given to the requests we make for things agreeable to the will of God. It surely is no hard or grievous condition that is attached to the blessings He bestows, that we ask for them; while you must feel satisfied, that, in the very nature of things, prayer is a fit means for keeping alive in our minds a constant sense of our dependence on God, and cherishing those holy affections which qualify us for the reception of the Gospel, and make us meet for the inheritance of the saints in light. Can a higher honour be bestowed on mortals than being permitted to enter the sanctuary of God, and worship Him who is adored by angel and archangel. In every act of true spiritual worship we leave behind us the ignoble attachments of earth and ascend to those mansions of glory where Jehovah has fixed his throne. We come into His immediate presence, we behold all His excellence and hold friendly and affectionate intercourse with Him. Thus seeing Him as He is, we become more intimately acquainted with His nature and attributes, with the requirements of His law, and assimilated to Him who is the express image of His person, and in our nature has revealed the Father unto us. And when our thoughts return to the necessary cares and duties of this world, like richly freighted vessels from a distant land, they will return fraught with the spirit that pervades every bosom in heaven with love to God and love to all mankind. Like the influence of the example of those with whom we associate, we may not at once perceive the efficacy of prayer, yet it will always be attended with similar effects, and, more especially, if our supplications have been that His Word may have free course and be glorified. Indeed we can hardly imagine that they who have bent before the throne of grace, and earnestly implored a blessing on the labours of their pastor, will retire from the services of the sanctuary without being better members of society, better prepared for the duties of life, and better fitted for the kingdom of heaven. The voice, the manner, the matter of the preacher's discourse may not be to their taste, but they go not to find fault, but to profit by his instructions; their humility will lead them to consider whether much of what they dislike may not be attributable to their own ignorance or vitiated taste; while candour will constrain them to acknowledge that even from the most commonplace discourse much might be gathered, and, if appreciated as it ought to be, would largely contribute to their spiritual edification and improvement, and, much more than they who had neglected the means and opportunities they possessed could reasonably hope to receive. The infinite importance of the respective duties of pastor and people will beget a mutual sympathy, which will, in him, be manifested by intense earnestness in feeding the flock of Christ, and in approving himself faithful in the trust reposed in him by the Chief Shepherd and Bishop of souls; and, in them, by an anxious desire to grow in grace and in likeness to Christ, under the ministrations of His Word.

The simple habits and incidents of pastoral life have often been employed by the moralist to give point to his lessons and interest to his tale. I know no moral picture half so lovely, nor half so interesting, as that of the faithful Christian shepherd and his flock journeying through this dark, rugged, and dangerous world to the land of uprightness. Peacefully they proceed, fervently imploring heaven's blessings on each other, and lending each other mutual comfort and aid; he, carrying the lambs in his bosom, carefully removing every obstruction from the path, and gently freeing from the briars and thorns those that are entangled by the way; they, listening to the voice of the shepherd and following his steps as he goeth before them. This is no ideal picture. It is one that may be realized over the broad expanse of the world by the united faith-fraught prayers of pastor and people. Come, auspicious day! for then, indeed, would the tabernacle of God be with men, and the reign of heaven commence, which the sure word of prophecy teaches us to expect, when the light of the Gospel shall illumine every land, and the dark and dreary regions of superstition and error shall rejoice and blossom as the rose.

Perhaps I may be indulged if I take this opportunity of referring to a topic, somewhat in connection with what we have said, but perhaps more personal than ought to proceed from the pulpit; but, if the observations which I am about to make may, in any degree, contribute to draw more closely the bonds which unite us together, and stir us up to the exercise of mutual forbearance and charity, I shall neither think they are mis-timed nor that they degrade the sanctity of the place where I now stand. It may be said that, if I conceive it to be the duty of a pastor to remove, in so far as he is able, every obstruction that stands in the way of the spiritual edification of his flock, and well knowing that a general prejudice exists against discourses being read from the pulpit, to act consistently with my opinion, I should endeavour to mandate my discourses and avoid casting a stumbling-block in the path of the halting. This, I am now unable to do. The time taken in mandating a discourse I would consider more profitably employed, both for myself and the people I instruct, in acquiring a more extensive knowledge of Scripture truths, and, in so far as lies in my power, in composing clear, well-connected and interesting discourses, and I am persuaded, from the enlightened and liberal sentiments which my hitherto limited intercourse has led me to believe you entertain, that those who differ from me in opinion will bear with my deficiencies. Yet, I hesitate not to declare,—and this confidence rises to assurance, if you yield yourselves frequently and fervently to the duty enjoined in the text, and which I humbly crave on my own behalf, as well as on behalf of all the preachers of Christ's glorious Gospel that this you will do. Brethren, I beseech you, pray for us. Pray for us, I beseech you, by all that is interesting and beautiful in the spectacle of a company of dependent mortals bending in prayer before the throne of their

Almighty Father and Friend for things agreeable to his will; by all that is ennobling in the service; by all that personal satisfaction which is felt from the consciousness of the honour and dignity conferred in being permitted to approach into the presence of Him before whom angels veil their faces with their wings, as unworthy to look on His uncreated glory. Pray for us, by all that pure and exalted delight which the benevolent heart experiences in the exercise of charity and love. We think it a mark of friendship, and we take a noble pride in recommending one in whom we have an interest to one by whose patronage and support he may rise to honour and distinction in the business of life. But who is greater than the Eternal Ruler of the universe—the Father and the Friend of the good—and what greater honour can we have than being permitted to commit those whom we love to His protection and care. Pray for us, I beseech you, by the salutary effects which this act of worship will have on your own tempers and dispositions, and by the close and intimate connection which subsists between it and the salvation of your own souls. Time is fast fleeting onward, and bears with it on its wings the most momentous consequences. By its shortness and uncertainty, and all that is awful in the contemplation of death, judgment and eternity, I beseech you, pray for us. It is now called to-day with you. Mutability and vicissitude are stamped on everything earthly; and the lessons which this fact is silently pouring into the ear forcibly remind us of the necessity of being up and doing. Another period by which the lapse of time is marked will soon draw to a close. The shadows of a few more evenings shall fall and the dawn of a few more mornings will lighten the world, and the present year will be numbered with the ages that are past and gone. But who can say that he will see the end of the coming year? Those who to-day are blooming in beauty, and in the buoyancy of health may calculate on a long life, may, ere to-morrow, be cut down as a flower of the field, and in a few days their bodies may be crumbling into dust. Such considerations should have, at all times, a powerful effect on minds capable of serious reflection. From these considerations permit me to urge you to the necessity of working out your salvation with fear and trembling, while time and opportunities are mercifully given you. From these considerations let me urge you to be frequent suppliants at the throne of grace, pleading that God would give you that living faith—for it is his gift—that, in answer to your prayers, will bring down plentifully the richest of heaven's blessings on your souls, and on the souls of all those with whom you are connected by any tie. Let these exhortations sink into your minds, and may these precious fruits be exhibited in your conduct. And, O thou Almighty hearer and answerer of prayer, while I crave the prayers of this people for a blessing on the Gospel of salvation, which I am sent to preach unto them, and that grace may be given me, that in all my ways I may glorify Thee, and finish with acceptance the work Thou hast given me to do, hear Thou, in heaven, and grant an answer to their prayers in peace, and bless abundantly the preaching of Thy holy Word, that it may have free course on the earth and be glorified! And to THEE, Father, Son, and Holy Ghost, one God, be all the glory.—Amen.

SERMON II.*

GOD CREATED MAN IN HIS OWN IMAGE, IN THE IMAGE OF GOD CREATED HE HIM; MALE AND FEMALE CREATED HE THEM. AND GOD BLESSED THEM, AND GOD SAID UNTO THEM, BE FRUITFUL, AND MULTIPLY, AND REPLENISH THE EARTH, AND SUBDUE IT: AND HAVE DOMINION OVER THE FISH OF THE SEA, AND OVER THE FOWL OF THE AIR, AND OVER EVERY LIVING THING THAT MOVETH UPON THE EARTH.—*Gen.* I, 27, 28.

MY FRIENDS,—It must, I think, be evident to you all that there is an intimate connection between the condition of man, as stated in the first of these verses, and the blessing pronounced upon him in the second. In other words, that man's power to subdue the earth and his dominion over the irrational tribes of creation depend on his being created in the image of God. It is to God-like man dominion is committed, to man created in God's own image that authority is given. The Divine image is the title to his power and prerogatives, his God-like nature fitted him for

---

* Preached before the Synod, at Hamilton, Ontario, on Sabbath, the 6th June, 1869.

accomplishing his high destiny as lord of creation. Our text, therefore, embodies the great constitutional law of man, and determines the purposes of his being. He is to be "fruitful and replenish the earth," *i. e.*, he is to people the fair scenes of this sublunary world with multiplied images of intellectual life, and moral beauty, united in one community, by the sacred ties of divine love. He is to " subdue the earth," *i. e.*, he is to make himself acquainted with those subtle and tremendous forces which the Creator has stored up in the physical world, and make them the subjects of his God-like will.

Obedient to the fixed laws imposed on them by the Creator, these latent forces, evolved, controlled and directed by God-like benevolence, would minister to the wants and wishes of man, and everywhere spread before his delighted eyes scenes of paradisaic loveliness and peace; but under the sway of a malevolent will in their impetuous energy would rend the earth to its deepest foundations and destroy every vestige of order and harmony. God-like man, by a thorough knowledge of their organic laws, would modify, combine and regulate these forces, so as to make them the obedient servants of his enlightened and holy will; would make them the communicating medium of his authority over the irrational creation, both animate and inanimate, and appropriate their various properties to his own use; would make them the exponents of his will, the medium of communication with all spiritual intelligences, with angels, yea, and with the eternal fountain of thought, the ever living and uncreated *One*.

This constitutional *law* seems to have been re-established at man's second birth, but with some modifications. When the earth emerged from the purifying waters of the deluge, beautiful as the hues of the rainbow—that seal of the covenant which bound afresh the agencies of nature to the destinies of man—God blessed Noah and his sons, and said unto them: Be fruitful, and multiply, and replenish the earth. And the fear of you, and the dread of you, shall be upon every beast of the earth, and upon every fowl of the air, and upon all that moveth upon the earth, and upon the fishes of the sea; into thy hand are they delivered. We may here remark that the subjection of the earth is not expressly specified, or, in other words, the dominion of its latent forces was not committed to man. The fear of him and the dread of him was to be on all inferior creatures, and into his hands they were committed, but not, as formerly, that he might rule them with absolute sway. Why was this? Because he is no longer the holy and benevolent being he originally was. The image of God is defaced in his soul. He has lost the dominion of the physical world because he is no longer like unto God, by reason of which likeness sovereignty over the earth had been committed to him. He is now unfit to hold the reins of authority, even had they been put into his hands. The principles of his nature are now at variance. Intellectually he is unable to discern what is good. Morally, he is unfit to rule. The propensions of his nature are not now purely benevolent, nor can his intellectual, his moral and physical powers be so fused as to produce unity of action. What would be the result, I ask, if, in his present ungodlike condition, he held the latent forces of nature at his command? What would be the result, if, with his heart teeming with every hateful passion, he could enjoin the thunders, and guide the lightnings, and charge the powers that upheave the earth, and make the mountain smoke, to obey his will? These forces in his hands would be fearful implements of destruction. In his instinctive and selfish struggles for dominion all that is morally beautiful and good would have long since perished from the earth. Man warring with man would have convulsed the universe. His enlarged mental energies would have augmented and made more formidable the implements of evil, and everything capable of destruction would have long since sunk in the conflagration of unholy passions.

Let us here for a moment inquire what the image of God in man is that fits him for dominion over the earth and the creatures that are therein.

There seems to be a threefold division in the nature of man, i. e., the whole man is composed of three several parts: the soul, or the moral and religious nature of man; the spirit, or pure intellect — reasoning — conscience; the body, the material tabernacle in which these powers dwell, and by which visible expression is given to their unseen actings. It is understood, says a popular writer of our day, that Paul makes allusion to this distinction of parts when he prays for the Thessalonian Church, that "the whole spirit, soul, and body be preserved blameless unto the coming of the Lord Jesus Christ." No doubt, says he, man is thus composed, whether the division be good or bad, or whether the Apostle alludes to it or not.

It is the constant, united and harmonious action of these several parts or principles of man's nature, and not the exclusive exercise or predominating power of any one of them, that fits man for dominion. Each one must occupy its own sphere of action, and not encroach on that of the others, or rather, there must be a perfect unity in their individual actings. There must be goodness, wisdom and power operating as an undivided whole, a complete and perfect fusion of these distinct principles in every determination of the human will. It is the unity of the divine attributes that forms the grand characteristic of the government of God. It is the unity of the moral and intellectual principles expressed through the material part of his nature that constitutes the image of God after which man was created. There have been high developments of mind in the world, wonderful manifestations both of skill and power, since the creation; but, in them all, it will be found that these principles, though they have operated in combination, have not acted in unity. But without unity of purpose and of action they will be inefficient elements in working out the destinies of man. They have wanted the harmonizing, fusing element of heavenly love. Not, indeed, wanted it entirely, otherwise the world could not have stood, but they wanted it in that due proportion which would have checked their irregularities, which would have assimilated their energies and directed them to their legitimate ends. They wanted goodness, the principle by which the power and wisdom of the Superior Ruler of all things is regulated and directed. They wanted that *love* by which He binds all His faithful subjects in allegiance to His throne; by which He unites in holy brotherhood all the children of men; by which He elevates and sanctifies human thoughts and desires, and by an amazing economy fits the family of earth for a holy incorporation with the great family of heaven. They all wanted, as a pervading element, a supreme regard to the will of God, which constitutionally belongs to humanity, but has been so obliterated as scarcely to be legible in any of the pursuits or actions of men.

We cannot take even a cursory glance at the great events of the world's history without having the conviction forced home upon us that it is not physical power, nor the might and energy of pure intellect, nor of intellect and physical strength combined; it is not the ethereal dreams of imagination, nor the brilliant conceptions of genius, nor the exquisite manipulations of art, ministering to the refined pleasures and voluptuous indulgences of social life, that elevates humanity, and gives it the mastery of the world. These, indeed, are elements in the process, elements that hitherto have been chiefly in operation, but, astonishing as the fruits have been, no experience of the results can convince us that, alone, they will ever replace the lost sceptre of dominion, in the hands of man.

And, yet, in these days, when mechanical powers and intellectual vigour have apparently reached the culminating point of excellence, and the world's progress is advancing with the lightning's speed —when the widening fields of knowledge have enlarged both the views and resources of men, and one discovery leads the way to another of greater magnitude and importance with a rapidity that is absolutely bewildering, and ominous of results that baffle the human mind to conjecture; he would indeed be a bold speculator who would affirm that the final result will not be the highest state of perfection, and the elevation of man to his lost throne of dominion over the forces of nature. Already, in the vastness of his power, he seems to have reached almost the culminating point of his high destinies. Even now, he flies over the earth with the speed of the winds. "Fire and vapour of smoke," waft him over the seas. "He sends the lightnings that they may go," and obedient to His command, they say "here are we."—He hath measured the heavens; and weighed the worlds that career through unbounded space! By the application of His skill, He has ascertained the component parts of many substances, and the laws which give to each, its particular form, and weight, and colour: and with a sovereign hand He presses them all into His service Look at the steam engine, what a mastery of mind over matter does not only its nicely moulded form, but also its complicated and accurately adjusted movements, display! Look at the gallant ship, in the face of the angry winds and boisterous waves, careering over pathless waters, guided in her course by a knowledge of the magnetic attractions of a needle; and impelled by the application of a simple mechanical power! Look at the earth returning in richest abundance of fruits and flowers, the labour and fertilizing properties which a knowledge of its component parts enables the skillful agriculturist to supply? Is it now deemed incredible that the whole earth and sea shall be girdled with a line of intelligence; or that any undertaking, however stupendous, can defy the powers of man? We recently spoke with hopeful confidence of spanning the broad St. Lawrence with an iron pathway, on which self-impelling vehicles would rush along with marvellous velocity. That is not now a doubtful problem. It is an accomplished fact! And man, in the consciousness of his skill, smiles at the idea of the enraged river, heaving its icy mountains with a mightier force than that of the thunder-bolt at the light and beautiful structure, that seems to smile defiance to its power. The accelerated progress of knowledge verifies the maxim that "knowledge is power." But what limitation can we assign to that power in relation to human agency? It would be vain to conjecture! Most of the tremendous forces, that man, with sovereign power, now presses into his service, are but of recent discovery; and their attributes are but in the process of development. Although they have been operating since the birth of time, yet, they are but as yesterday to man. But what great things, even in the infancy of his acquaintance with them, have they enabled man to achieve? When these, and all the other forces of nature, perhaps some of them still undiscovered, shall be fully developed—when man himself shall be thoroughly permeated with divine goodness, comprising in that term every moral attribute; when he shall have all his powers, mental and physical, perfected, and harmoniously attuned, and it shall be a necessary law of his being, to modify, combine, control, and direct the mighty agencies of nature to the most beneficent moral purposes, then shall the earthly destinies of man be accomplished, and the will of God shall become the sole law of sanctified humanity. But until this renovation is effected, assuredly we need not expect that the Eternal King will commit to man, as his vice-regent, the unlimited command of the latent forces of nature.

These elements, to be effective of any thing truly great and good, must be regulated and controled by a God-like will. Physical strength and intellectual power may be employed to a bad as well as a good purpose. Like a sword in the hand of a madman, high intellectual power, in the possession of a godless man, would be a fearful and destructive implement. Was there a universal diffusion of knowledge; were the highest attainments in the mechanical arts reached by every man; were men intellectually and physically equal, those distinctions of rank observable amongst us, and which seem essential to the very existence of society now, would be unknown, and every man would do that which is right in his own eyes. But would there be peace and plenty? Would there be prosperity and happiness? Would there be those cherished feelings and affections which belong to families? No! We fearlessly affirm that there would be universal anarchy, and a disorganization of society, more complete than occurred in the world before the flood! and destruction more awful. A licentious spirit of self-government, of which we now see the incipient evils, would pervade individual minds. Each one would struggle for sovereignty! Each one would be his own ruler. Each one would be a god, a god unto himself, a god over all others. Each one, impelled by the laws of his constitution, would aim at universal sway. Increased mental energies, and enlarged physical powers, would be sources of more tremendous evils than have yet fallen upon man, and in the fierce contests for dominion, the human race would be extirpated from the earth.

Man is not yet prepared for his original birth-right of dominion. He is not prepared for living with his race in unity, equality, and fraternity, and this is indeed a condition of his being in a state of perfection. The process is going forward that will effectuate it. But intellect and physical strength, as we have said, are not the sole formative principles. They are indeed the mightiest instruments now at work; but were they mightier than they are, they would be incapable of giving effect to the great constitutional law of man. God-like benevolence is just as essential a part of that law, as knowledge or power. There must be, moral, intellectual, and physical energy, in united and harmonious combination. In a word—the reformation within him of the image of God, before he can regain or expect to regain his birthright sovereignty.

Now, is there any thing that would lead us to suppose that man will ever regain the possession of his lost dominion? Shall his knowledge ever be so enlarged as to apprehend the nature of every thing material, and know intimately the laws by which their mutual relations are determined; and have the power to dispose and arrange them according to his will; shall he ever become God-like, and obedient to the *first* law of his nature; shall he of necessity choose good and reject evil—mastering the latent forces of nature, shall he ever be able to compel them to submit to his sovereign sway? This may seem a visionary expectation. But when we announce this as man's *destiny*, we are borne out in the assertion, both by the testimony of heaven and earth.

The divine economy revealed in the books of nature and inspiration is professedly a plan for restoring man to his birthright privileges by restoring him to the image of God. The history of the world in all the departments, both of animate and inanimate nature, is demonstrably but a narrative of this plan, advancing step by step to its consummation.

We cannot even take a cursory glance at the intellectual and moral condition of the human race in connection with the great events of the world's history, without observing the silent, slow, but steady progress of mental development—without observing the germs of thought, at first struggling into light through ignorance of the high purposes of God, and man's immortal existence—that, like cimmerian darkness, settled down upon him at his fall—and then, in efflorescent beauty, presaging its profounder attainments in scientific truth. Nor can we fail to observe that the practical and beneficial results of increased mental power, had depended on and corresponded most exactly with the developments of another principle—religious truth—which has been gradually evolving since the day that the promise was given, that "the seed of the woman shall bruise the head of the serpent." Nor can we look at the progressive power and transforming effects of this principle without entertaining the confident anticipation that it will ultimately expand, enlighten, and purify the human mind and fit man for again holding the reign of sovereign authority over the forces of creation.

If we look to the mental developments of the earlier ages, as exhibited in the remains that have come down to us of these sciences and arts, we cannot fail to be struck with the influence which religious truth had on the production of these results. An attentive observer of facts must perceive that all the loftier exhibitions of mental skill owe their origin to the silent influences of religion. This is sufficiently attested by the structures of India, of Egypt, and even of Greece, while the disintombed ruins of Babylon and Nineveh testify to the same truth. It is admitted that a deep veil of mystery still shrouds from the inquiring the circumstances that gave origin to these stupendous structures, the very descriptions of which fill us with amazement allied to incredulity. It is only through the rendings of that veil which time has effected that we can dimly see and imperfectly read these legends. But from the shivered parcels of knowledge which we can collect, we are warranted in concluding that in these nations the mighty impulsive power which operated on the public mind and educed the national resources for the construction of these sublime embodiments of their inner spiritual conceptions was religious truth. We can trace in them all a recognition of the existence and supremacy of God—of a belief in man's immortality, and his proud aspirings to a higher than his earthly destiny. This shews plainly that the religious sentiment lay at the foundation of all the great movements in history, if not in the form of a cherished sacred feeling, yet, as an instructive propelling power.

More especially the revelation of the will of God recorded in the Gospel of Christ throws the clearest light on the present condition and future prospects of man. It intimates in strong terms his coming dignity and sovereign power. It tells us that he shall "reign with Christ," "for whom are all things, and by whom are all things." It asserts, what every man must feel whose moral sense is not utterly vitiated and whose conceptions of God are raised above the most brutal ignorance, that he has fallen from his original state of innocence; that the image of God in his soul is defaced; that, instead of being a ruler, he is a degraded slave; at the same time it makes known a plan by which his sins are all taken away, their guilt pardoned, and he is re-created after the image of God in Christ Jesus, and refitted for the high purposes of his being.

The word of God has gone forth into the world fraught with divine power, and it "will accomplish that for which it is sent."

On minds that "receive it in love of it," the spirit of truth and holiness is operating with a quickening, sanctifying power. It is making the ungodly like unto the Son of God himself, holy, good, and utterly free from selfishness and sin. Though the leaves of the *Bible* in themselves, and apart from the living spirit that is operating through them, are as inefficient to any good purpose as the dry leaves which the autumn winds shake from the trees, yet, containing, as they do, "the testimony of God, concerning His Son," the truths recorded in them become "spirit and life unto every one who receives them in faith. The Gospel of Christ "is the power of God and the wisdom of God unto the salvation of all who believe," and divine power and wisdom will assuredly affect that great change in the moral and intellectual condition of man which will fit him to appropriate the latent forces of nature, and to employ them for the accomplishment of the great ends of his spiritual and immortal life.

The renovating power of the Gospel is progressive and irresistible. It is silent and unseen, and can only be known by its effects; but, as it operates through a visible agency, we can easily discern these effects, and they have been greater and more astonishing than the most marvellous transformations in the material world. Men who have lived in all manner of wickedness have been made holy and good. Men who have hated God and each other, by the transforming power of divine truth have become God-loving and devout, meek and gentle, tender-hearted and kind; in a word, have been made like unto the Son of God, who came into the world to do the will of His Father, and went about continually doing good, both to the souls and bodies of men. Such is the natural tendency of a loving reception of the truths of the Gospel. They exalt, purify, and spiritualize the nature of man; they restore within him the image of the invisible God.

In the Gospel, not only are the most perfect instructions given, but, also, the most finished and perfect pattern of every virtue and every grace is presented. In Christ Jesus we behold, embodied, that exalted excellence to which all shall be raised who believe in Him, "for in Him dwelleth all the fulness of the God-head bodily," *i. e.*, in the Man Christ Jesus all the attributes of God, in perfect union with humanity, are manifested. The incomprehensible God, whom no eye hath at any time seen, is revealed in a condition which our finite minds can comprehend and appreciate; "all the goodness of God is made to pass before us. And O how glorious is the spectacle! In the Man Christ Jesus, we behold infinite wisdom and goodness administering infinite power! All-embracing love directing unsearchable knowledge! How consistent with each other, and with the whole will of God, was His every thought, every word, every action! How loving and compassionate! How holy, and just, and true! How tender, and kind, and good, was He! His character was unique. No one ever approached it by an infinite degree. Truly, He was God manifested in the flesh.

And yet, it is to such perfect excellence that the Gospel designs to raise the sinful children of men! By faith they are united to Christ, and the glory which the Father hath given unto Him He hath given unto them, that they may be brought to "a complete communion of Divine life with Him." When the grand scheme revealed in the Gospel for the moral renovation and redemption of man will be completed, they will be assimilated to Him, and raised to a share of His happiness and power, for He hath declared, " to him that overcometh will I grant to sit with me on my throne, even as I also overcame, and am set down with my Father on His throne."

When man shall have all the powers and faculties of his nature, both mental and physical, thus perfected and harmoniously attuned, and it shall be a necessary law of his being to modify, combine, control and direct the mighty agencies of nature to the most beneficent moral purposes, and the will of God shall become the sole law of his thoughts and actions, then shall his earthly destiny be accomplished. Then, this rudimentary state of things shall close, " and a new heaven and a new earth, wherein dwelleth righteousness, shall be the dwelling place of holy, spiritualized humanity." Intellectual life shall then consist in choosing that which is good, and applying the best means for the accomplishment of the best ends. Moral life shall consist in absolute purity, in constant action. Physical life, in the exercised functions of a spiritual, immortal body. These, in union, will be the distinguishing qualities of perfected humanity. The living power of the Gospel of Christ, having accomplished its great transformations, man shall be re-invested with his lost sovereignty, and shall reign with Him who is head over all things, for ever and for ever.

The blessed spirits around the throne of heaven, in their song that is ever new, are represented as ascribing glory and praise unto Him who redeemed them by His blood, and made them unto their God, kings and priests to reign with Him on the earth. It is far beyond the powers of our minds even to conceive the blessedness of those who, as kings, shall reign over the tremendous forces that are stored up in nature, and as priests shall present them all, an offering unto God in the accomplishment of His will. The triumphs of mind over matter which we now behold are, so to speak, but the germinal buds of the matured fruits of mental grandeur in those happy scenes which shall succeed this perplexed and troubled state of being—a state of being, however, perplexed and troubled though it be, which is, perhaps, the one best adapted for eliciting the faculties that fit a man for the society of heaven—best adapted for making him acquainted with those forces, and the organic laws they observe, on the knowledge of which his future intercourse with the spiritual world depends. Forces which annihilate time and space, and the command of which invests man with a power, the results of which it is impossible for him, in his present state, even to conceive.

In conclusion, permit me to offer a few exhortatory remarks by way of inducing you to cultivate with care your physical, your moral, your intellectual faculties, and to strive to have all the principles of your nature so elevated, purified, and harmoniously adjusted, as to fit you to " reign with Christ upon the earth ;" and as priests, to present the various motive powers of matter, with the governing laws and results, a holy offering unto God.

No physical culture, it is true, can give life,—that is the gift of God, through the Lord Jesus Christ. The body is the casket in which that gift is preserved; and the instrument by which its operations are expressed. By observing the laws necessary to health and longevity, you give an enlarged sphere, and a more intense energy to the actings of your moral and intellectual nature.

Although the spiritualized body, when it is raised from the dust of death, shall in many respects differ from the body of flesh in which we now live, we have no reason to believe that any of its powers or faculties shall have perished in the grave. These are essential elements of humanity, necessary to its perfected condition as well as to its growth and maturity. It is by physical action that the thoughts and desires of the mind are expressed. The more perfectly they are expressed the more true and sympathetic will be the contact of one mind with another, and less liable to misapprehension or error. In our ignorance of the future we cannot tell what effect the full development of our physical powers will have on our spiritual condition, but, assuredly, the results will be glorious. This we know, that while striving to perfect them we are doing the will of God, and, as His agents, carrying forward the great work which He is accomplishing on the earth.

Cultivate with care your intellectual powers, endeavour to form the habit of accurate observation and patient thinking. Many things will occur in the journey of life which you know little or nothing about, but their causes and effects it is important you should know. Let nothing that is new to you pass from your minds without becoming the subject of patient scrutiny. Many individual and social advantages are derived from this practice. The simplest incidents oftentimes give origin to the most important discoveries. The falling of an apple to the ground led Newton to reflect on that power which causes all bodies to descend to the centre of the earth. Investigating this power on the principles of sound philosophy, he discovered the law of universal gravitation, a discovery which wrought such a revolution in the opinions of men, as to present philosophy in a new aspect, and religion in a more attractive form. It will not be till all the latent powers and properties of nature be fully elicited and distinctly understood, that man's earthly destiny shall be accomplished and humanity fitted for the employments of the eternal world.

Above all cultivate your moral and religious nature with assiduous care. If we have been correct in our deductions, that the sentiment of religion, either as an instinct or a moral principle, has been the chief stimulus to every great enterprise in the ancient world, if the utility of every discovery has wonderfully corresponded to the developments of this principle; if, until it is perfected, and God's will shall be the sole law of our lives, we will hope in vain to repossess our birthright dominion over the earth; if without this principle to regulate the outgoings of knowledge, our acquirements would be a curse instead of a blessing, O then cultivate your religious sentiments with peculiar care. To this end you have every advantage given you; you have divine instruction given, a perfect example set before you, heavenly aid promised you, and the noblest object that can inspire ambition and animate Christian zeal is placed before you as the end and aim of all your aspirations. Let the mind that was in Christ be also found in you. Until you are made like unto Him, you are unfit to guide the elements of nature, and command them to obey your will.

Science is increasing its bounds, knowledge is enlarging its fields of operation. The world of mind and the world of matter seem to be hastening to perfection; why should the Divine science of knowing God in Christ stand still? Why should the fields of heavenly knowledge remain uncultivated? Why shut our eyes to the light of the truth, that alone can guide our course over the dark waters of perplexed and troubled thought? Why shut our hearts to the influences of God's love, which would mould them unto His own image and make fallen man like unto Christ Jesus, holy, benevolent, ever doing good, whose voice all nature obeyed; whose will was the will of His Father in heaven, whose dominion endureth throughout all generations.

When man, created anew after the image of God, shall be pure, righteous and good, as when first he came from the hands of his Maker, and shall offer the fruits of his enlarged faculties an holy offering unto God, then shall be completed the great work which Christ came from heaven to accomplish. You are called to be fellow-workers with Him. If noble ambition can inspire your hearts with courage; if glory, honour, and immortality can excite you to patience and perseverance in well-doing; if eternal life be a reward adequate to the dignity of the renewed mind, the prize is before you. The most favourable advantages are afforded you, the Sabbath with its holy ordinances, communion with God and its blessed influences, the Bible and its words of perfect life and liberty are the high privileges you enjoy, Christ is ever with you to make them available. Yield yourselves to the influences of His Spirit. Through Him strengthening you, you can do all things you will attain dominion not only over the earth but the higher glory of ruling your own spirits, being filled with the light and the righteousness of God. Amen.

SERMON III.

AND IT WAS WINTER.—*John* X, 22.

THE winter is a season that is fitted to call up reflections of a solemn but of a peculiarly interesting and improving kind. The year, closing amidst its rigours and when nature seems dead, silently leads the mind to the time when the long and dreary winter of death shall come, and the darkness of the grave shall cover us. But, if winter is associated with the gloomy thoughts of death, it is also brightened with the pleasing hopes of immortality. If we give the parting tribute of a sigh to the departed year, that may have borne away with it many of our joys, so do we hail with gladness the advancing year, which, in the buoyancy of hope natural to the human mind, we expect will be fraught with many blessings. As these anticipations come crowding upon us, if we devoutly raise our thoughts to that gracious Being, " from whom cometh down every

---

This, the last sermon preached by Dr. Mathieson, was one of his favourite discourses. It appears to have been written about the year 1848, and to have been preached frequently—twice at least to the Congregation of St. Andrew's—the last occasion being on the 23rd of January, 1870.

good and perfect gift," the winter would not only remind us of the close of human life, but would also lead us to contemplate those scenes which shall succeed the fluctuations and changes of mortal existence, and for the enjoyment of which the trials and vexations of this passing scene are wisely and graciously designed to be preparatory.

We are now in the very heart of the winter. The light and the heat of the sun are diminished; the day " has dwindled to its shortest span;" the earth is buried beneath the snow; myriads of those living beings that sported in the beams of the summer's sun are motionless or dead, and others have taken their flight to more congenial and far distant climes; the groves are now silent, or echo to the moaning winds; the rippling streams, which lately to the imagination seemed the very types of youthful gaiety, are now ice-bound and still, or like a mighty giant, contending with death, for a moment they struggle with their crystal fetters, and then, " like a child that has brawled itself to rest," they lie still and silent as death. Over the face of nature a death-like torpor is cast, and scarcely a vestige of what clothed hill and dale with beauty is now to be seen. Yet, over this dead and desolate scene the bright and beautiful sunshine is often thrown with surpassing splendour, like the light of immortality shining on the coldness and desolation of the tomb. The jocund voices of congregated friends, in healthful exercise on the ringing ice or crisping snow, the glad re-unions of the scattered members of families around the paternal hearth, the warm flow of charity, brimming over to the cold and hungry poor, which this season calls forth, may remind us too that there are affections and feelings which death cannot destroy; that spiritual life glows amidst the desolation and decay of matter, and of that joyful re-union of the far scattered members of the great family of God, when time shall be ended and eternal ages shall run.

Nature lifts up her instructive voice in every season, and adapts her lessons to the varying emotions of every period of human life. But never is her voice more awfully solemn, nor her lessons more important and instructive, than when uttered amidst the storms and ravages of the closing year. To the consideration of these, our text naturally directs the thoughtful mind, but in calling your attention to the teachings of Nature it shall not be our object in this discourse to lay before you all the lessons suggested by the text, interesting and important though they may be. We will confine our observations chiefly to the circumstances with which it is connected, and hope that, by blending them with the emotions that naturally belong to this season, a deeper and a more permanent impression of divine things may be made on our minds, and that the storm and desolations of the winter may be unto us the impressive preachers of righteousness.

It was winter. This was the season when the Son of God appeared in the world, and the cold and bleak aspect of Nature is a befitting emblem of the cold and uncourteous reception that was given to Him by those He came to save. He came to his own; but his own received him not. Though He was "the Lord of Glory," "the Prince of the Kings of the earth," none welcomed His advent—none waited to do Him homage; He seemed an outcast in the world, which He Himself had made. He was despised and rejected by the creatures He had formed. The hardships and privations to which He was exposed cannot be surpassed in the condition of the most neglected of the children of poverty, even amidst the rigours of the most inclement winter.

Brethren, our hearts are touched with pity when we look upon the sufferings of homeless poverty and want aggravated by pinching cold; and colder than the bitter blasts of the winter must be the heart of that man who would not to the poor, at least to the suffering poor, extend relief. Judging from these generous feelings of our nature, we can hardly conceive it possible that we could have incurred the reproach which is justly attached to the Jews, for their inhospitable reception of the Saviour. But let us bear in mind that much of this generous sympathy with the suffering poor must be ascribed to the benign influences of the religion of the Son of God. an advantage which the Jews possessed not, and that much of their unkind treatment of Jesus arose out of prejudices with which we have not to contend. But notwithstanding our superior advantages, have we any reason to boast of a more profound sympathy with the "Man of sorrows?" Have we given Him a kinder reception than His own ungrateful countrymen gave Him? When He sent out His disciples with the messages of peace and salvation He said unto them: "He that receiveth you receiveth Me." This is great plainness of speech. Have His messengers come unto you in His name, and with His own gracious words of love and mercy on their lips, and have you received them as you think you would have received Jesus, the Son of God, had you lived when He was manifested in the flesh? Have you listened to them with the same intense earnestness as you think you would have listened to Him "who spake as never man spake" had you enjoyed the privilege of listening to the audible tones of His heavenly voice? It is vain to say the case is altered now; that those who come to you are rude in speech and ungainly in manners; they tell you nothing that you have not heard before. Christ knew well what He said, and we repeat His words, " he that heareth you heareth Me." He well knew that those He sent forth with the overtures of pardon and peace were men full of imperfections and sin, that the " bodily presence" of some of them " was weak" " and their speech contemptible," yet He selected such imperfect earthly vessels for the conveyance of the messages of His love, and He claimed for *them* in the exercise of their holy duties the same honour and respect that should be shewn to Himself. " He that despiseth you despiseth Me, and he that despiseth Me, despiseth him that sent Me."

Brethren, if we would bear in mind these solemn words of our Lord there would be surely less disrespect shewn to the messengers whom He sends, and less indifference to the tidings which they bring. Surely if we felt that we were condemned sinners, and hell was yawning to receive us, our cry would be, " what shall we do to be saved" Instead of seeking to have our ears tingled, and our tastes gratified, we would earnestly seek to have our hearts affected, and would listen with the most intense interest to every illustration, and to every exposition of that scheme of mercy and grace by which the sinner is sanctified and saved. Our earnest desire would be to have the life-giving truths of God's Word dwelling richly in our hearts. It would not be for the streams of worldly delight we would thirst, but for water from the wells of salvation; and we would drink of them deeply, whether presented to us in an earthen cup or in a golden chalice.

But what is the reception that men generally give to the messengers of Christ? Is it with the "enticing words of man's wisdom," or in the unadorned simplicity of truth that they desire to have the Gospel preached unto them? There is no disguising the fact, unless the Messenger of God come with all the artificial graces of oratory, and a voice in modulated tones to captivate the ear, he will not meet respect due to his sacred office. What is the reception they give to the divine message itself? Do they who hope to be saved by the faith of the Gospel cherish its truths in their own hearts and endeavour to have them extended and established in the world? "The foxes have holes," said our blessed Lord; "the foxes have holes, and the birds of the air have nests, but the Son of man hath not where to lay his head." Like its homeless Author, Christianity still seems to want shelter and a resting place in the world. What has been done for teaching and making disciples of all nations of the earth? This is the mission of kingdoms as well as individuals, but what provision has the most favoured kingdom made for the maintenance of the public worship of God, and publishing the knowledge of salvation throughout the world? Apart from political considerations, absolutely nothing. As a fiscal arrangement, as a cheap state police, the preaching of the Gospel is sanctioned, and in some states publicly supported in some measure. The tendency of Christianity as a national institution is to promote the peace and prosperity of society, to empty the prisons by preventing crimes, to diminish pauperism by promoting industry, to establish interna peace by inculcating contentment and the practice of good morals, and to effect these important purposes, in some places, a little has been given, but stintedly and grudgingly. But, in relation to men's higher and immortal destinies, what have nations done for the establishment of Christianity on the earth? O, cry out some, with affected earnestness, "the kingdom of Christ is not of this world;" it has no connection with its policy or pursuits. A national religion corrupts the streams of divine truth. A national church letters the free spirit of Christianity, encroaches on the civil liberties and religious privileges of the people. The work of evangelizing the world has been committed to the saints. The duty is fours. We perform the commandment of the Lord. Ah! "What meaneth, then, this bleating of the sheep in mine ears, and this lowing of oxen that I hear?" If it is the duty of one and all of Christ's followers to devote themselves and all that they have unto Him; if this dedication of themselves be a free and voluntary self-sacrifice, what mean, then, those blatant appeals from platforms and pulpits to the generosity of "the Christian people." What mean those bellowings and boastings of what has been reserved from luxurious pleasures as sacrifices unto the Lord? After all the noise and pious prattle that has been made, what are these sacrifices? crumbs from the table! paltry clippings of garments! the sweepings of fraudulent gains perfumed ostentatiously with the odour of charity!! Has there been a sacrifice of spiritual pride? of sectarian animosity? of Pharisaic arrogance? Has there been a willing obedience to the "exceeding broad commandment of Christian love" which is better than all sacrifices. Brethren, calmly and candidly, contemplating the state of Christianity in the world and the efforts that have been made to extend the boundaries of Christ's Kingdom, can we affirm that either Christian nations or Christian men have done their duty? Has even the Church been faithful to the trust committed to it? We are obliged to confess that, like its unnoticed and neglected Author, Christianity still sleeps as in a manger; that it is still confined as with swaddling clothes, and is benumbed by the chilly wintry blasts that whistle around it.

2ndly. "It was winter." This was the season, says the Evangelist, somewhat emphatically, when Jesus walked in Solomon's porch, in all probability to shelter Himself from the inclemency of the weather, as well as indirectly to give the Jews another proof that He was the Messiah.

In all the sinless infirmities of humanity Jesus participated; He submitted to hunger and cold and fatigue in the execution of the work given Him to do. In the porch, or covered way of the Temple named after the Son of David, did Christ, his Son in a far higher and spiritual sense, seek to shelter Himself from the merciless blast; but cold and cutting as it was, it was not so keen as the storms which the malice of his enemies, caused to fall on his unsheltered head.

It is painful to think that this storm continues to rage with unabated fury. We speak not now of those who openly blaspheme His holy name, and with demoniacal fury attempt to subvert His heavenly religion, we speak of those who profess to honour Him, but who in their deeds deny Him. As sincere inquirers after truth, the Jews came round about Him, asking Him to tell them plainly if He were the Christ. This seems to be a reasonable and a candid request; but their hearts were full of prejudices and animosity against Him, which no testimony could subdue. Had He told them plainly that He was the Messiah, we know from the subsequent context what would have happened.

He told them, as plainly as the state of their own hearts would permit the truth to be revealed, consistently with the natural accomplishment of His purposes, that all power in heaven and in earth was His, that life and death were in His hands, and He accompanied these declarations with such proofs of His veracity as were sufficient to convince reasonable men; but they believed Him not. His humble birth and His obscure condition did not correspond with their notions of the Messiah. And when He asserted, in express terms, His divine origin and heavenly power, they accused Him of blasphemy, and would have stoned Him to death had He not " escaped out of their hand."

How similar is the conduct of many professed followers after truth in these days, to that of the Jews. They come to the Bible with the ostensible question, tell us plainly, is Jesus of Nazareth the Christ but their judgment is already formed. They believe that he is merely a man, it may be a good man, qualified to instruct mankind how they may enter into the kingdom of heaven. To every Scripture testimony to these facts they yield their assent, but when, in very explicit terms, the Bible affirms that Jesus has power in Himself to lay down His life, and to take it again; when it speaks of his death as an atonement for sin, and ascribes an efficacy to His blood that is more precious than all created objects; when it testifies that salvation is God's work entirely, and refers to the manifestations of God in nature and in providence as a proof that its revelations are true; when it speaks of the utterly helpless state of all mankind, and that none but Jehovah can save them; when it ascribes the incommunicable attributes of Jehovah to Jesus, and asserts His being one with the Father, in terms which no sophistry can mystify, and no ingenuity can subvert, they are driven to denounce the views, which an honest, unbiassed mind would take of these statements, as blasphemous, or to have recourse to unbelief. These sufficiently plain testimonies of the Bible are all so irreconcilable with their pre-conceptions of the nature of God, and the laws of his moral government, that they will not believe them. Our Lord tells us why: "Ye believe not" said He to the Jews, "because ye are not of my sheep. My sheep hear My voice and they follow Me, and I give unto them eternal life." They, like the Jews, have formed a scheme of salvation, more in accordance with what they think to be right and philosophical. They are wedded to their own notions. It is not with the spirit of candid inquirers that they approach the Scriptures. Instead of listening to their testimony, as that testimony would be received by simple-minded and candid men, they listen to the suggestions of their own reasoning faculties, and follow the counsels of their own hearts. Though they know but few of the ways of Jehovah and cannot comprehend the full thunder of His power, yet they would concentrate in their own narrow minds all knowledge of His nature and attributes, and denounce as blasphemous everything that would controvert their own limited views of His incomprehensible nature, and unfathomable purposes.

But it is not by the blasting influence of speculative opinions, inconsistent with the plain and simple statements of God's Word that men corrupt and destroy the genuine fruits of the Gospel; by their practical indifference to the doctrines of Christianity, there is more real harm done, than by open hostility. "If ye love Me," said Jesus, "ye will keep My commandments." If obedience be the test and measure of love for Jesus, few, I fear, can free themselves from the reproach of treating Him disrespectfully, as the unfeeling Jews did. Which of His commandments have been faithfully kept? Who, with corresponding zeal, have striven to advance those great purposes which He came into this wintry world to accomplish? Have we ourselves done nothing to retard His religion, or excite against it the withering scorn of the scoffer? Have we never, by our indifference to the all-important truths of salvation, confirmed others in sin or encouraged them to pursue the path that leads to destruction? I fear, brethren, even when we drop the tear of morbid sympathy over the memorials of His sufferings, were we faithfully to remember how we have discharged our incumbent Christian duties, we could not adduce our fidelity to His commandments, as an evidence of our love to Jesus. Our hearts are often as cold as the winter's snow to all that tends to advance His kingdom, and the tenour of our conduct is as injurious to vital godliness as the bitter blasts from the frozen north are to the early flowers of the spring.

3rdly. Our thoughts are directed by our text to the circumstances which distinguished the season when Jesus walked in Solomon's porch. "It was at Jerusalem, the feast of dedication, and it was winter."

The feast of dedication was not of divine appointment, it was instituted long posterior to the giving of the Law, probably by Judas Macabeus, and afterwards confirmed by the supreme counsel of the nation. It was designed to commemorate the recovery of Jerusalem from the heathen, and the purification of the Temple from the gross profanation of it by the impious Antiochus. Either out of revenge or cruel policy, that tyrant, after quelling an insurrection in Jerusalem, slew 40,000 Jews in one day, and sold as many more for slaves. Not contented with this, he profaned the Temple in a way most abhorrent to the religious feelings of the Jews. He intruded himself into the "Holy of Holies," into which it was unlawful for any one but the High Priest to enter, and only lawful for him, once a year, when he entered with the blood of atonement. To pollute the sacred edifice, to the utmost degree, he caused swine to be sacrificed on the altars of God, and water in which the flesh of these unclean animals had been boiled to be sprinkled on every part of the building, that it might be rendered utterly unfit for the worship of the living God.

After it had lain three years in defilement, it was recovered by the Jews and purified with many sacrifices and lustrations, and dedicated anew to the worship of God. It was to commemorate the purification of the Temple that the feast of dedication was instituted. The Jews celebrated it with great pomp, as a resuscitation of their political being, and, as it were, life from the dead, and Our Lord sanctioned it with His presence.

But, brethren, the defilement of the symbolical temple was not more complete than the pollution of the human soul by sin. The soul is the spiritual temple of God, which at its creation was honoured with the divine presence, and which He hath promised to fill with His glory; but before the Spirit of God can dwell in the soul of man it must be purified, raised from desolation, and consecrated to the service of Jehovah. Like the material temple, it must be sanctified by sacrifice and lustrations, by the sacrifice of Him who "came to put away sin" by offering Himself unto God

SERMON III.

for us, and by sprinkling the soul with His blood, which "cleanseth it from dead works to serve the living God."

Without straining the analogies of nature beyond due bounds, does not the winter, with its softly falling snow, suggest lessons of spiritual purity and divine activity, analogous to what both reason and Scripture tell us must pass upon the soul of man, before it can be restored to the divine favour? As winter approaches, the earth gradually assumes a deadlier aspect, a more sombre hue; yet still there is vegetable life and matured beauty. Many of the autumn's flowers are in bloom; the meadows are still green, and the tinted leaves still adorn the woods. It is winter: they droop and die. The first nipping frost strips the flowers of their beauty and sweeps the leaves in rustling showers to the ground. The earth is cold and dead: incapable of sustaining life: rugged and unsightly. The fleecy snow descends, how soft and beautiful! almost imperceptible, like the breath of the Spirit, wrapping, as in a winding sheet of transparent whiteness, the wan face of dying nature, and clothing in robes of purity the memorials of decay. White robes are given to every one of them, and it is said: "Ye shall rest yet for a little season." They disappear from the earth, but it is to burst forth again in renewed and resplendent brightness.

"What are these that are arrayed in white robes, and whence came they?" "These are they that have come out of great tribulation, and have washed their robes and made them white and clean in the blood of the Lamb. Therefore are they before the throne of God and the Lamb, and serve Him day and night in His Temple."

The heavenly purity of the saints of God is not perfected till the winter of temptation and trouble is over and gone. It is out of great tribulation they pass into glory. When the storms and tempests of life are past, purified from sin, they shall enter into the joy of their Lord. Like the flowers of the field in the winter's storms, every earthly virtue shall perish amidst the trials of faith; all selfishness shall wither; the soul shall be clothed with the robe of the Redeemer's righteousness. But though all that is earthy shall die, the seeds of spiritual life, that were matured amidst corruption and decay, shall survive, and through the life-giving power of Christ's death shall again be called into activity. They will arise in the image of God, after which they were originally created.

This renewing of the whole man must be begun on earth, though it will only be completed when the winter of death is past, and the genial mildness of eternal spring shall be diffused over the wide sphere of spiritualized humanity. Then, the bodies that are sown in corruption shall be raised in incorruption. But it is here the seeds of life must be deposited in the heart. The Spirit, like the breath of spring, will cause them to germinate and spring up, and bear their appropriate fruits.

To this spiritual cultivation we must here devote ourselves; we must open our hearts to the reception of the principles of holiness and truth, and wait in faith till the Spirit of God evolve them in beauty.

Among the many important lessons which the winter teaches, we are impressively admonished of the necessity of attending immediately to the duty of dedicating ourselves to the Lord. The heaven-appointed means are within our reach. They must be applied.

They can only be made effectual through the influences of the Holy Spirit. The Spirit will be given to them who ask for it, and, through faith, will impart a divine efficacy to the blood of atonement.

The Temple, desolate and polluted, without sacrifice, without songs of praise, the bleak winds of winter whistling through its deserted porches, and gloomy sky throwing a deeper shade of melancholy into its courts, empty, where the people of the living God did congregate. The polluting worship of devils, staining its desecrated walls, presented not to the Jew a more saddening spectacle than the unrenewed, unsanctified soul of man to one who is alive to a sense of his condition in the sight of God. Brethren, in the spectacle described in that passage of which our text forms a part, we have before us an objective representation of the purification of the soul of man, the living temple of the living God, and the divine glory with which it shall be filled.

Who is He that walks in that *Porch* of the material Temple, distinguished for its superior beauty, that is associated with the most glorious period of Jewish history, and is a pledge of the fulfilment of the promise, that the Lord " the Desire of all nations shall suddenly come into His Temple, even the messenger of the covenant?" It is Jesus of Nazareth, lowly and meek, with nothing attractive but His divine purity and benevolence! Who are these that throng around Him? They are the children of Abraham, who profess to seek the promised Messiah. Jesus tells them that He is He whom they seek, and He refers them to His works in proof of His veracity—works which none but God could accomplish. He is the Son of David, according to the flesh, and the lineal heir to the throne of Israel. But surely, a greater than either David or

Solomon is here. The once desecrated Temple was purified by sacrifice and lustrations, and is now blessed with His presence, who came into the world, as He tells them whom He addressed, to purify, by the sacrifice He was about to offer, the spiritual temple of God, and dedicate it anew to His glory. His work was to sanctify and save all who believed in Him, and give unto them eternal life. As the desecrated gold and silver of the material Temple was purified by making it to pass through the fire, and the polluted garments of the priests, by being thoroughly washed, so, by the fiery test to which their faith was exposed, and by washing them from sin in His own blood, He would thoroughly cleanse all who believed in Him, and fit them for offering unto God holy and acceptable sacrifices. He would sit, as His Prophet said concerning Him, as a refiner of silver, "and will purely purge away their dross and take away all their tin."

The present is the time for these fierce trials of faith, the time of purification, and for dedicating ourselves to the service of the Lord. The time is short to us all for the performance of these indispensable duties. It will be soon ended; but if we are not sanctified by the blood and Spirit of Christ, and fitted for glory before the winter of death come upon us, we must perish. Like the green herb, before the deadly blasts of the wintry storm, our hopes shall be strewed in the dust, never to be revived by a returning spring, but buried in the desolations of an eternal winter.

The reflections to which the winter gives rise are in beautiful harmony with the spirit of reformation which the children of God are called to cultivate, and the hopes of a blessed immortality which they will delight to cherish. Brethren, let these reflections lead you to begin and follow out with firm purpose, a more active course of faith and duty; strive, by those means by which God has promised to communicate the sanctifying power of His Spirit, to have your conduct purified from those stains of sin which a conscientious inspection of your past lives will reveal. There is not one among us all, who, on looking back, can say there is nothing in his conduct he would wish to amend, nothing that he has left undone, nothing that he would desire to alter. Wherefore, brethren, let us humbly repair to the throne of grace, through the new and living way opened up to us, to implore grace to purify us from all ungodliness, and to help us to devote ourselves unreservedly and for ever to the service of God.

There are many other important and instructive reflections suggested by the words "and it was winter" which we have not had time to touch upon. We have confined ourselves to those chiefly suggested by the circumstances connected with the text; with Divine permission we may at another time take up some of them, and endeavour to draw from them those lessons of encouragement and hope which they are so fitted to teach.

May God bless what has now been said in accordance with His will and conducive to His glory. May the emphatic expression "and it was winter" remind us of the coldness and neglect of men to their own eternal interests, of the love and sufferings of the Redeemer, and teach us to die daily to sin, and dedicate ourselves unto God holy and living sacrifices, "which is your reasonable service."

Now to the King Eternal, immortal, and invisible, the only wise God, be all glory and praise. AMEN.

CONCLUDING TRIBUTE.

At a public breakfast given in Montreal, on the 4th of June, 1870, to the Synod of the Church of Scotland in Canada, the absence of the venerable minister of St. Andrew's Church was felt by all present. In his reply on behalf of the City Clergy, Dr. Jenkins feelingly alluded to his departed brother, on whom would undoubtedly have devolved the duty of acknowledging the honour, done to the Synod had the entertainment been given a year before, while Dr. Cook of Quebec expressed his affectionate remembrance of his deceased friend in these terms,—

"One thing it is impossible to refrain from remarking, the absence from among us of that noble form, which even amidst the frailties of declining years, and under the pressure of domestic calamity, imparted a certain dignity and respectability to all our ecclesiastical assemblages, connected as it was, with an independent judgment, with consistent principle, and with a genial and loving nature, cast in the true Scottish mould, and cherishing such persistent and unwavering attachment to his country and his country's church, that it might be truly said of him in the words of the Psalm,—"their very dust to him was dear." I am not now to pronounce an unqualified eulogium on Dr. Mathieson. No man is altogether without faults and failings. But, take him all in all, it will be long before the citizens of Montreal or the members of the Synod of Canada, look on his like again. It is well known that I often differed from him in church matters. There were others of the brethren, with whom in regard of these, I sympathized more. But he was my first friend among the ministers of Canada, and to the last day of his life, he held the first place in the regard and affections both of myself, and of the members of my family."

www.ingramcontent.com/pod-product-compliance
Lightning Source LLC
Chambersburg PA
CBHW021346230426
43666CB00006B/422